Foods of the Lebanon

WITHDRAWN

Foods of the

Lebanon

CASSIE MAROUN-PALADIN

PHOTOGRAPHY BY JOHN PEACOCK

NEW HOLLAND

Introduction

If you have two pennies, buy a penny's worth of bread for your body and a penny's worth of jasmine for your soul.

I T IS WITH FOOD that the Lebanese express hospitality, and the sharing of meals plays a large part in the Lebanese way of life. Cooking in Lebanon is an intricate, inherited art, inseparable from the history and traditions of its people. When celebrating special occasions such as weddings, christenings and birthdays, the food that is served is of huge significance, and great care is paid to every element of the meal. For days beforehand, family and friends work together to prepare the feasts that accompany these festivities, each person contributing a dish that is their own particular speciality.

Even in the course of day-to-day life, welcoming guests into one's own home by offering them something to eat and drink is almost obligatory. To persuade someone to stay for a meal is an honour for the household as well as the guest. Extra food is always prepared in case of unexpected visitors and a variety of dishes can invariably be produced at very short notice. A strict code of etiquette governs the occasion. One never asks guests why they have come, but receives them with pleasure, greeting them with the welcoming words '*Fadlah, ah la ouh sahla*'. The host then enquires about the members of the guest's family and gives blessings to each of them. For the guest's part, he or she is expected to decline all offers of food or drink (no matter how severe their hunger!) but the host will ignore these refusals and serve an array of irresistible morsels. Throughout the meal the guests praise the food and the hosts, and the phrase '*is mis salib*' – which wards off the evil eye – is frequently spoken, followed by '*sahteyiye*' (bon appetit).

A typical Leabanese meal is not a three-course affair based around a plate of meat and vegetables. Instead, diners are offered a variety of small dishes from which to help themselves. Hors d'oeuvres, known as mezze, exemplify this way of eating. To the Lebanese, mezze are a way of life. There are more than 80 dishes that can be served in this way, but a typical spread will include a few carefully selected dishes, well balanced

Green bean stew with lamb (p. 79) and Lebanese bread (p. 22).

in colour, taste and texture. The best known and most popular are kibbi, tabbouleh, meat or spinach pies, stuffed vine leaves, olives, pickles and dips made from aubergines, avocados or chickpeas. The dishes are served with flat bread, and it is customary to put some herb sprigs on the table. A colourful and attractive spread is an intrinsic part of the pleasure of eating mezze.

Elaborate desserts are not common, and most people will simply end a meal with some fruit or yoghurt. But that's not to say the Lebanese don't have a sweet tooth – delectable pastries and sweetmeats, fragrant with rose or orange blossom water and drenched in syrup, are often served with coffee during the day.

The Lebanese cook is spoilt for choice when it comes to ingredients. Lebanon covers a long strip of mainly mountainous land, but the coastal strip and lower slopes of the mountains have a Mediterranean climate and are served by abundant springs – ideal conditions for growing fruit and vegetables. Crops are grown at varying heights on the mountain slopes, often on terraces and, because the climate changes with the height of the land, anything from bananas to apples can be grown successfully. Livestock such as poultry, goats, sheep and cattle are also kept.

National dishes make the most of this rich local harvest. The use of vegetables is widespread – whether fresh in salads, cooked in stews or preserved as pickles. Aubergines are especially popular, as, of course, are olives. Dried pulses, rice and grains such as couscous, cracked wheat and semolina provide bulk, and plenty of fresh Lebanese bread is always on the table.

Yoghurt is one of the most versatile of ingredients and is added to soups, stews and desserts or made into a refreshing iced drink.

Aromatics are a trademark of many Arab cuisines and Lebanese dishes are liberally seasoned with all kinds of herbs, spices and flavourings. Mint and parsley, cinnamon and cumin, rose water and lemon juice are just some of the flavours used to enhance the ingredients of a dish. Nuts are traditionally added to dishes both sweet and savoury – particular favourites are pine nuts, almonds and walnuts. Fruits such as figs, dates and apricots are used in sweetmeats and preserves, usually after being dried, which gives them an intensity of flavour and ensures they are available all year round.

Lebanese cooking is economical. Most meat dishes use mince or cheap cuts of meat that have to be cooked slowly, and stews usually contain a large proportion of vegetables, pulses or grains, making small amounts of meat go further.

Just as Lebanese food must be served in the correct manner, its preparation is also important. Among the older generation particularly it is a labour of love – much of a woman's day used to be spent preparing the family's meals, involving time-consuming tasks such as making bread and pastries, filling and folding tiny pies, stuffing kibbi and pounding meat. Today, labour-saving devices such as blenders, food processors and pressure cookers, as well as the availability of ready-prepared ingredients, have done away with much of this hard work and, thanks to freezers, many dishes can be prepared in advance, at a time that suits you.

Like all traditions, the art of Lebanese cooking is passed down from one generation to the next – few recipes have to be followed religiously and each family has its own way of cooking its favourite dishes. My family is no exception. Many of the recipes in this book were handed down to me by my grandmother, who taught me to cook and nurtured my love of good food. Other family members and friends have also contributed. Over the years I have added to, amended and adapted many of these recipes to suit my own tastes, to bring them up to date or to make them easier to prepare. I have given alternative ingredients wherever possible but find that, as interest in the cuisines of other nations grows, unusual ingredients are becoming easier to find. Large supermarkets now stock most of the items I have used in my recipes, while ethnic shops or delicatessens should have the more specialist ingredients. It's worth a little effort to seek out authentic raw materials and give yourself a true taste of Lebanon. 'God's bounties are beautiful. Let us enjoy them while there is still time.'

Menu planning

BREAKFAST IS USUALLY a miniature affair consisting of hors d'œuvres such as cheese, yoghurt, olives (mainly black), Lebanese bread or toast with clotted cream and preserves. Sometimes a fried egg in butter or a hard-boiled egg is prepared. There is usually a zaatar (thyme and cumin) mixture on the table. Breakfast is rounded off with coffee.

The main meal of the day used to be served at lunchtime, but in accordance with modern lifestyles, is now served in the evenings. There is always an hors d'œuvre served with a drink beforehand.

Page numbers refer to recipes.

Lunch
meat pies (p. 28)
tomato and cucumber salad dressed
    with oil, lemon juice, salt
    and pepper (p. 108)
bread (p. 21), olives (p. 19) and
    cheese

Dinner
green bean stew with lamb (p. 79)
rice with vermicelli (p. 43)
tomato salad (p. 108)
yoghurt (p. 32), fruit and coffee

Lunch
omelette with courgettes (p. 61)
yoghurt (p. 32)
bread (p. 21), olives (p. 19) and cheese
fruit and tea or coffee

Dinner
rice with chicken (p. 45)
chickpeas with sesame paste (p. 105)
tomato salad (p. 108)
fruit, cheese and olives

Lunch
cracked wheat salad (p. 112)
yoghurt (p. 32)
fruit and coffee

Dinner
baked fish in sesame sauce (p. 53)
rice
plain fried aubergines (p. 91)
green salad
fresh fruit and coffee

Lunch
grilled meat (p. 70)
cabbage salad (p. 111)
bread and sliced tomatoes
fruit and coffee

Dinner
yoghurt soup (p. 40)
stuffed courgettes (p. 97)
stuffed aubergines (p. 94)
fresh fruit and coffee

Lunch
potatoes with chickpeas (p. 89)
avocado salad (p. 111)
bread (p. 21), cheese, olives (p.19)
    and coffee

Dinner
noodles with lentils (p. 34)
yoghurt (p. 32)
fresh fruit
sweetmeats (p. 146–151)
coffee

Lunch
stuffed vine leaves (p. 101)
baked kibbi (p. 66)
cucumber with yoghurt (p. 104)
coffee

Hafla – A party or celebration.
Have a finger meal where all the
hors d'œuvres can be prepared
beforehand. Most of them freeze
well. Set the table the day before
and enjoy your party!
    Here are a few suggestions:
pickled turnips (p. 13)
pickled cucumbers (p. 14)
pickled onions (p. 17)
pickled sweet peppers (p. 16)

Arrange the pickles attractively
on a platter. Chop parsley, mint
and basil leaves together and
sprinkle over the pickles to
add colour. Slice tomatoes and
arrange overlapping around the
edge of the plate. Place a slice
of fresh cucumber on each

tomato round and sprinkle with
chopped parsley and paprika.

meat pies (p. 28)
spinach pies (p. 30)
avocado salad (p. 111)
chickpeas with sesame paste
    (p. 105)
aubergine with sesame paste
    (p. 107)
hard-boiled eggs with cumin
    (p. 58)
fried fish (p. 48)
Surround fish with little bowls
    of taratoor (p. 49)
fried chicken (p. 82)
raw kibbi (p. 64)
Surround kibbi with lettuce
    leaves and place a basket of
    bread next to it.

baked stuffed kibbi (p. 66)
stuffed vine leaves (p. 101)
stuffed cabbage leaves (p. 102)

Bread is an integral part of a
finger meal and should be
placed within easy reach. On
another table place an urn of
boiling water and coffee,
Turkish delight and sugar-coated
almonds (these can be bought).

Try and make the following
treats beforehand:
semolina cookies (p. 130)
Lebanese lovers' shortbread
    (p. 132)
Pile these in a pyramid,
sprinkling lots of icing sugar on
each layer.
filo pastry (p. 141)

pickles

L ET US START with pickles as they take a while to mature. No Lebanese home is without
a selection of pickles. They are always served with hors d'œuvres as their colours add
gaiety to the table. Foods were originally pickled to preserve them, but as pickles are so
delicious anyway, they are served as hors d'œuvres and as accompaniments to main dishes.

The method of pickling is simple. Raw, fresh vegetables are soaked in brine – a
solution of salt and vinegar made according to individual taste. Salt and acid help to
ferment and mature the vegetables.

For successful pickling, all jars must be scrupulously clean and well-sterilized. If
possible, use glass tops – if not, cover the mouth of the jar with greaseproof paper and oil
the lids. There must be no air bubbles in the jar. The traditional method of testing if there
is enough salt in the solution, especially for olives, is to float an egg in the mixture. Mix
about 1.5 litres (2¾ pints) of water and 45 – 60 ml (3 – 4 level tbsp) of salt and bring to

the boil. Remove from stove and add a raw egg. Part of the eggshell, about the size of a small coin, must protrude above the surface of the water. If the egg sinks, more salt is needed. When cool, remove egg and add vinegar, depending on your taste for sourness. Equal amounts of vinegar and water or 300 ml (½ pint) vinegar to 900 ml (1½ pints) water is a fairly standard solution which does not make your teeth edgy or your mouth numb. But, as stated before, this is a matter of personal preference.

If pickles are preferred with a more sour flavour, use more vinegar and less water. Use young, fresh and unblemished vegetables. Most vegetables should be unpeeled or partially peeled. Wash and scrub them well. The pickles in the jar must always be completely covered with brine and the lid tightly sealed until maturity. The lid must be oiled.

mai-mal-ha

brine

The proportion is 1.5 litres (2½ pints) of liquid to 1 kg (2¼ lb) of vegetables unless otherwise stated.

MAKES 1.5 LITRES (2¾ PINTS)

1.1 litres (2 pints) water

400 ml (¾ pint) vinegar (use white wine vinegar for clear pickles)

45 – 60 ml (3 – 4 tbsp) salt

Mix all ingredients together in a clean glass or china container. Optional extras, which enhance the flavour, are celery leaves, celery stalks, garlic, dried red chillies, bay leaves and black peppercorns.

khal

vinegar

You can make your own vinegar from grapes. Save all the stems and any grapes which are not good enough to eat. Mash the grapes and put them, with the stems, into a large pottery jar. Each time you have leftover grapes, add them to the jar.

Keep in the jar for 2 – 3 months. Squeeze out juice, strain and mature in bottles for a year. If red vinegar is wanted, add some red grapes.

Previous page: Pickled onions (p. 17); Mixed pickles (p. 13); Pickled cabbage (p. 14).

kabees l'ft

pickled turnips

These have a very distinctive flavour, but are so delicious that they don't take much getting used to. The taste is enhanced by the beetroot, which also adds a lovely cerise colour to the dish.

MAKES 2 X 1 KG (2 LB) OR 1 X 2 KG (4½ – 4¾ LB) JARS

1 kg (2¼ lb) turnips, unpeeled
1 – 2 beetroot, peeled

2 – 3 cloves garlic (optional)
1 – 2 chillies (optional)
5 ml (1 tsp) whole black peppercorns (optional)
1.25 litres (2¼ pints) brine (see p. 12)

Scrub the turnips. Cut the turnips and beetroot into large chunks. Press the pieces snugly into sterilized glass bottles, adding the garlic, chillies, and peppercorns if using, alternating layers of turnip and beetroot. Cover with brine and seal. The pickles can be eaten within a few days but should not be left for longer than a month.

kabees meshakel khala't

mixed pickles

Most of the pickles that are prepared the same way can be put together into a large jar. Here is a rough estimate of amounts:

MAKES 2 X 400 ML (¾ PINT) JARS

2 large carrots, thickly sliced
1 small cauliflower, separated into florets
250 g (9 oz) pickling cucumbers
250 g (9 oz) small turnips, unpeeled
1 green pepper, thickly sliced (remove pith but add seeds)

1 celery stalk, cut into chunks
3 – 4 cloves garlic
1 – 3 hot chillies
2 – 3 small beetroot, peeled and quartered
15 ml (1 tbsp) pickling spice
5 ml (1 tsp) black peppercorns
brine (see p. 12)

Prepare as for pickled turnips (see above). Leave for 2 – 3 weeks. Refrigerate these pickles and they will last for more than 2 months.

kabees arnabeet wa koronb

pickled cabbage

Cauliflower may also be added to this pickle for a slightly different taste and texture.

MAKES 2 X 400 ML (¾ PINT) JARS

1 beetroot, peeled and sliced
1 cabbage, cut into chunks
1 hot chilli (optional)

black peppercorns
1.25 litres (2¼ pints) brine mixture
    made up of 900 ml (1½ pints) water,
    300 ml (12 fl oz) white wine vinegar,
    45 – 60 ml (3 – 4 tbsp) salt

Wash vegetables well and put into a glass bottle. Add chilli and peppercorns, cover with brine and seal. Store for about 10 days, preferably in a warm place.

kabees kh'yaar

pickled cucumbers

MAKES 2 X 400 ML (¾ PINT) JARS

750 g (1¾ lb) pickling cucumbers
4 – 6 cloves garlic

few sprigs fresh dill
2.5 ml (½ tsp) black peppercorns
3 – 4 coriander seeds (optional)
brine (see p. 12)

Scrub cucumbers and put into a glass jar with rest of the ingredients. Cover with brine and store for 10 days.

kabees marboyseh banadoura

pickled tomatoes

MAKES 2 X 400 ML (¾ PINT) JARS

6 slightly unripe tomatoes

280 g (10 oz) fine table salt
lemon juice
750 ml (1¼ pints) olive oil

Wash and dry tomatoes and cut in half. Place in a glass bottle, sprinkling each with a layer of salt and lemon juice. Cover with oil and seal. Store for about 10 days.

Lebanese breakfast of mixed pickles (p. 13), cheese, Avocado salad served as a dip (p. 111),
Traditional bread (p. 22) and a Fried egg (p. 57).

From left to right: Pickled cucumbers (p. 14); Black olives (p. 20); Pickled turnips (p. 13).

kabees batenghen

pickled aubergines

MAKES 2 X 400 ML (¾ PINT) JARS

1 kg (2¼ lb) long, thin aubergines
100 g (4 oz) walnuts
2 cloves garlic

salt
1 bunch of parsley, finely chopped
1.5 litres (2¾ pints) brine (see p. 12)
olive oil

Prick aubergines all over with a fork. Poach in boiling salted water for 5 – 10 minutes until just tender. Drain. Make a small incision along each aubergine. Crush the walnuts and garlic with the salt and mix with the parsley. Use to fill the slits in the aubergines. Pack into sterilized jars. Pour in brine to cover and add enough olive oil to fill the jar. Seal and store for at least 10 days. Shelf life is 2 months, longer if refrigerated.

VARIATIONS

- Omit the walnuts and mix 4 cloves of garlic and 1 or 2 chopped dried chillies with the parsley.
- Instead of covering the aubergines with brine, use half brine and half olive oil.

emma's filfil

emma's pickles

I would like to give you another method which, although not Lebanese, is too good not to pass on. Emma was a very good Afrikaans-speaking friend of mine at whose home I have eaten many a good meal.

MAKES 2 X 400 ML (¾ PINT) JARS

1 kg (2¼ lb) red and yellow peppers	6 bay leaves
6 cloves garlic	salt, to taste
5 ml (1 tsp) black peppercorns	2 – 3 hot chillies
	olive oil
	white wine vinegar

Wash peppers and leave whole. Wrap each in foil and bake in an oven at 180 °C/350 °F/Gas 4 for 30 minutes. Cool and slice. Pack into sterilized jars with garlic, black peppercorns, bay leaves, salt to taste and hot chillies. Add equal quantities of oil and vinegar. Refrigerate. Can be eaten almost immediately.

olives

Lastly, the monarch of all pickles. They involve a lengthy process, but if you have eaten home-pickled olives, you will realize they are worth every bit of the preparation.

Green or black olives are a matter of preference; the method of preparation is slightly different for each.

zatoon eswid

black olives

MAKES 2 X 400 ML (¾ PINT) JARS

2 kg (4¾ lb) raw black olives
280 g (10 oz) coarse salt
125 ml (4 fl oz) white wine vinegar

few cloves garlic
15 ml (1 tbsp) pickling spice
few hot chillies
few sprigs thyme
125 ml (4 fl oz) olive oil

There are other methods of pickling olives but, believe me, this is the best one. If you don't wish to go through this lengthy process then use the second recipe.

With a sharp-pointed knife, slit each olive down one side. Cover with cold water and leave to soak for 17 days to eliminate bitterness. Change water every day. Then soak in salt water (tested with the egg method, see pp. 11–12) for 3 days, stirring every now and then. Drain.

Soak for 3 days in 1 part vinegar and 2 parts water, ensuring that the olives are covered at all times. Drain and add garlic, pickling spice, chillies and thyme. Pack in sterile jars and pour on oil to cover. Seal and leave for at least 4 weeks. The oil eventually gets a distinct olive taste and can be used for kibbi and salads.

2 kg (4¼ lb) raw black olives
280 g (10 oz) coarse salt

125 ml (4 fl oz) olive oil
125 ml (4 fl oz) brown vinegar

Slit olives down one side and wash in warm water. Cover with cold water and soak for 6 – 7 days, changing the water every day. Drain. Put olives into sterilized glass or earthenware containers. Combine salt, oil and vinegar. Pour over olives, seal and leave for 3 – 4 weeks. They can be eaten sooner if you don't mind the bitter taste.

zatoon akhdar

green olives

MAKES 2 X 1.4 KG (3 LB) JARS

2 kg (4¼ lb) green olives
150 g (5 oz) salt
2.5 litres (4½ pints) water

lemon wedges
1 – 2 hot chillies (optional)
brine made by boiling 1 litre (1¾ pints)
water with 280 g (10 oz) salt

Instead of slitting the olives, crack them with a mallet or a clean, small hammer, being careful not to crush them. Combine salt and water and cover olives. To prevent olives floating to the top of the solution, place a plate on top. Leave for about 6 weeks, changing salt water once a week. Drain the olives and pack in sterilized jars. Put a few lemon wedges between layers and 1 or 2 hot chillies. Cover with cooled brine. Seal well. Leave for about 6 weeks.

breads & pies

THE PICKLES ARE now maturing so let's bake the bread. In Lebanon, bread is eaten at breakfast, lunch, and dinner, indeed, any time of day.

Lebanese bread is the most essential eating commodity. To scoop up kibbi, hummous, etc. with bread, or to wrap it around grilled meat with greens and spices, is sheer bliss. It is as traditional to eat with your fingers as it is acceptable for a member of the family to break bits of meat or chicken and pass them around by hand.

The smell of freshly-baked bread is a most satisfying aroma. How I loved to hover around when my granny was baking. She always made a special pitta for me, the butter melting in the hot, hollow pouch.

When we moved into our home many years ago, an Afrikaans friend of mine married to a Yugoslav, brought bread and salt when she visited the house for the first time, explaining 'the bread that we may never go hungry and the salt for luck'.

aysh shami

Lebanese bread

This version is like the Greek pitta. You can use Lebanese bread dough for a variety of recipes, such as oven pies (see p. 24), herb rounds with sesame seeds (see below) and onion bread (see p. 24).

MAKES 12 – 15 LOAVES

25 g (1 oz) fresh yeast or 1 sachet easy-
    blend dried yeast
5 ml (1 tsp) sugar
500 ml (17 fl oz) tepid water or 250 ml
    (8 fl oz) water and 250 ml (8 fl oz) milk,
    in which case boil the milk and allow to
    cool to tepid

750 g – 1 kg (1¾ – 2½ lb) plain flour
10 ml (2 tsp) salt
15 ml (1 tbsp) clarified butter or melted
    butter
15 ml (1 tbsp) olive or vegetable oil

If using fresh yeast, mix with the sugar and 250 ml (8 fl oz) of tepid water until it dissolves. Leave in a warm place until bubbly. Sift flour and salt into a bowl. Make a well in the centre of the flour and pour in the yeast mixture, butter, oil and enough tepid water or milk to make a soft dough. If using easy-blend dried yeast, just sprinkle into the flour. Work flour into centre of ingredients with hands, adding liquid as necessary. Dough must be soft, but firm. Using both your fists and heels of your hands, knead it until well blended, soft and pliable, but not sticky. Form dough into a ball.

Pour oil on the bottom of the dish, or oil your hands and coat the ball well, thus preventing the dough from becoming dry and crusty. Place the dough in a large dish with a lid or in a basin covered with a blanket. Leave in a draught-free, warm place (a warming drawer, which has been switched off, is a good place) for 1 – 1½ hours until the dough has doubled in size. Press the dough down in the centre and draw the edges to the centre to re-form the ball.

Turn onto a floured board and knead for about 1 minute. Break off small lumps about the size of tennis balls and flatten each ball on the floured board. The best way to do this is with floured fingers, but you can use a rolling pin. They should resemble small round plates (mine are any shape but round!). Place rounds on a lightly-floured surface, cover with a lightly-floured cloth and leave to rest for about 30 minutes. During this time the rounds should double in size.

Preheat oven to a maximum of 240 °C/475 °F/Gas 9. Heat baking sheets for a few minutes, sprinkle with flour, position bread rounds with 3 cm (1¼ in) between them and bake for 5 – 10 minutes. The breads swell in the centre as they bake. Traditionally they should not be brown, but I confess to preferring them very slightly browned. As they are removed from the oven the swelling will deflate. Wrap in a cloth or blanket. If you have enough to freeze, seal in plastic bags when cool. They are easily defrosted.

Previous page: Bread salad (page 107) and Spinach pies (page 30).

Do have one whilst still hot! Cut in half and fill the pocket with hard butter which melts into the bread. You cannot afford to have interruptions when baking bread, so leave your front door unlocked, as the smell of baking bread usually attracts friends and family.

The next time you have a barbecue, make a batch of dough and grill the bread instead of baking it. Butter the loaves as soon as they are removed from the grill. As each bread is buttered, put it in a saucepan and cover with the lid. I learned this tip from a very good Lebanese cook.

khoubz mar'uh
mountain bread

These are paper-thin rounds, up to 5 cm (2 inches) in diameter. You need to be energetic to make them, and I must confess that this is best left to the experts.

The tools you need for making this bread are a long-handled wooden spatula, measuring approximately 5 cm (2 inches) in diameter, or a round cushion. If you want to be daring, here is the recipe:

MAKES 9 – 10 LOAVES

Prepare dough as for *aysh shami* (see p. 22) leaving out the butter and oil. Roll out balls very thinly and then stretch them by throwing them between your hands several times. To get them really thin, cover a round cushion with a cloth and gently roll the dough. You can also use an upside-down wok. Bake as before, leave to cool, pack on top of each other and keep covered.
Fold and pack in plastic bags or containers with lids and freeze.

mahnoosh bi za'tar wa semsem
herb rounds with sesame seeds

Sumak is a shrub that grows in the Middle East. The leaves are dried and used as a herb, which has a tart taste. It is also used medicinally and for dyeing fabric. Lemon juice can be used instead.

MAKES 2 LOAVES

Lebanese bread dough (see pp. 22 – 23)
1 part thyme
1 part roasted sesame seeds
¼ part sumak or lemon juice
vegetable oil

Make a batch of Lebanese bread dough. When dough has been flattened, roll into saucer-sized rounds and leave to rest for 30 minutes before baking. Mix seasonings together. Make indentations with fingers in the top of the bread, pour oil over the surface and sprinkle over seasoning mixture. Bake at 200 °C/400 °F/Gas 6 for 15 – 20 minutes. Baked rounds must be soft in texture.

oven pies

MAKES 12 – 15

450 g (1 lb) minced meat
125 g (4 oz) cream cheese or drained yoghurt
  cheese (see p. 32)

Lebanese bread dough (see pp. 22 – 23)
melted butter

Fry the mince until browned and partly cooked. Mix with the cream cheese or drained yoghurt cheese.

Break off little balls of dough, flatten out to 3 mm (⅛ in) thick and 10 cm (4 in) in diameter, brush with melted butter and put some of the filling on the dough. Arrange on a pan and allow to rest for 15 minutes. Bake at 200 °C/400 °F/Gas 6 for 15 – 20 minutes.

VARIATION
■ Roll out each piece of dough paper thin, spread with melted butter, roll up into a long pencil, then form into a coil. Put some of the meat and cream cheese on top, let them rest for 15 minutes and bake in an oven at 220 °C/425 °F/Gas 7. Delicious!

khoubz basali

onion bread

MAKES 2 LOAVES

10 ml (2 tsp) easy-blend dried yeast
15 ml (1 tbsp) sugar
2.2 kg (5 lb) flour
250 ml (8 fl oz) lukewarm water

500 ml (17 fl oz) milk
30 ml (2 tbsp) salt
30 ml (2 tbsp) vegetable oil
25 g (1 oz) butter or margarine
1 – 2 onions

Dissolve yeast, sugar and 5 ml (1 tsp) flour in the water and leave for a few minutes until frothy.

In the meantime boil milk. Add salt, oil, butter or margarine and enough cold water to make 1.25 litres (2¼ pints) of liquid. Pour into a mixing bowl. Add flour and yeast mixture and, if required, add more liquid to form a soft dough. Knead the dough well. Cover and leave to rise, until dough doubles in size. This will take 1 – 2 hours. Knock back and, to obtain a really good texture, leave to rise again; then knock back, knead lightly and place in bread pans or roll out as required.

Slice the onions into thin rings. Embed the onion rings into the top of the rounds. Brush with oil and bake at 200 °C/400 °F/Gas 6 for 15 – 20 minutes.

Clockwise from top left: Onion bread (above); Lebanese bread (p. 22); Open Lebanese pies (p. 30); Herb rounds with sesame seeds (p. 23).

ageena

basic pie dough

MAKES 46 – 50

1 kg (2¼ lb) flour
10 ml (2 tsp) salt
30 ml (2 tbsp) vegetable oil

40 g (1½ oz) butter, melted
15 ml (1 tbsp) easy-blend dried yeast or
   15 g (¼ oz) fresh yeast
650 ml (1⅛ pints) warm water for mixing
oil for deep frying

Warm a large mixing bowl for a few minutes. Sift flour and salt into the bowl. If using easy-blend dried yeast, sprinkle over. Make a well in the centre of the flour. Add oil and butter (and fresh yeast if this is being used which has been fermenting). Mix well by hand mixing in enough of the warm water to make a soft, pliable dough. Knead dough for about 15 minutes.

Oil your hands well and rub over ball of dough. Cover dough with a damp cloth and set aside in a warm place to rise to double its size (1 – 2 hours). Alternatively, a large container with a lid is ideal for leaving the dough to rise in the switched off warming drawer of the stove.

fa'tay'yeh sanbusik

meat pies

MAKES 46 – 50

30 ml (2 tbsp) pine nuts (optional)
30 ml (2 tbsp) vegetable oil or 25 g (1 oz)
   butter
450 g (1 lb) lamb or beef, coarsely ground or
   finely chopped
1 large onion, finely chopped
1 small potato, grated (optional)

1 small tomato, skinned and grated (this
   makes it a bit more juicy)
salt and pepper
2 ml (¼ tsp) allspice
2.5 ml (½ tsp) cinnamon
5 ml (1 tsp) instant stock powder (optional)
lemon juice (optional)
basic pie dough (opposite)
oil for deep-frying

For special occasions, use pine nuts in this recipe. Heat oil or butter, add pine nuts and brown lightly. Remove with slotted spoon and set aside. Add meat to hot oil and fry for a few minutes. Add chopped onion and cook until soft. If using potato, add and cook for a few more minutes, stirring all the time. Add tomato, salt, pepper, spices and stock powder if desired. Turn to low heat and simmer until meat is cooked and juices absorbed. If using pine nuts, add after the meat is cooked. A little lemon juice may be added if you like.

Take small pieces of dough and flatten as thinly as possible with your fingertips, or roll dough and cut into rounds about 75 mm (3 in) in diameter. Place 15 ml (1 tbsp) of filling in the centre, fold over and seal. Place on a floured board. When ready to fry, heat oil and deep-fry until golden.

Clockwise from top: Cheese pies (p. 30); Spinach pies (p. 30); Meat pies (above).

fa'tay'yeh gebna

cheese filling

MAKES 24 – 30

450 g (1 lb) grated cheese – use any cheese:
    haloumi, cheddar, gouda or a mixture

2 eggs, beaten
pepper
pine nuts (optional)
basic pie dough (see p. 28)

Blend cheese with eggs and pepper. Use to fill the pies as described on p. 28. For special occasions, add fried pine nuts (see p. 28).

fa'tay'yeh b'sbaanegh

spinach filling

MAKES 24 – 30

1 kg (2¼ lb) spinach, washed, drained
    and chopped
1 small onion, finely chopped (or 5 large
    spring onions)
a few sprigs mint and parsley, finely chopped

2.5 ml (½ tsp) cinnamon
lemon juice
15 ml (1 tbsp) vegetable oil
pinch of allspice
pinch of ground cumin
salt and pepper
basic pie dough (see p. 28)

Mix all the ingredients well. (This mixture is also a family favourite as a salad.) Place 15 ml (1 tbsp) of filling on a round of dough, fold over and seal. Spinach pies are traditionally shaped like a three-cornered hat (see p. 27).

laham b'ajeen

open Lebanese pies

This is a lovely party recipe.

MAKES 20 – 24

Use the same basic dough (see p. 28). Break off pieces the size of ping-pong balls. Flatten well with finger tips. Have meat mixture (see recipe for meat pies, p. 28) ready. Add 250 ml (8 fl oz) yoghurt to this and lemon juice to taste. Cover rounds of dough with mixture, pressing into dough slightly, and put onto a baking sheet. Pour over the melted butter. Bake at 200 °C/400 °F/Gas 6 for 15 – 20 minutes, until crisp on the bottom. Serve hot. All bits of leftover dough can be pulled into a shape and fried.

yoghurt & soups

A LEBANESE HOME IS never without yoghurt – it is put on the table for all meals. Making it is a regular ritual and is an essential part of the daily Lebanese diet. We tend to take this health-giving nourishment for granted, even though it is strongly believed that daily consumption of yoghurt prolongs life and is recommended for sundry aches and pains. Enterprising is the person who had the good sense to market it. Unfortunately, this wholesome, delectable dish has been commercialized as a minor dessert and is usually synthetically flavoured. But there are many more uses for this versatile ingredient. Yoghurt can be used as a hot or cold soup, as a salad dressing or as a marinade. Yoghurt is delicious eaten with rice and vegetables, added to a gravy or on its own with bread. Serve it with *rishta* (see p. 34) and *m'jadrah* (see p. 42) or add to your marinades. A refreshing yoghurt drink, *ayran*, is sold in the streets of Lebanon (see p. 152).

When you realize how easy it is to prepare yoghurt, you will never buy the small, expensive, commercial containers again. Complicated equipment is totally unnecessary. All you need is a 'starter', or as the Lebanese call it, *raube*. Begin by buying a plain, live yoghurt – use the one in the 150 ml (5 fl oz) size. Thereafter, every time you make yoghurt you must top up your starter and store it in a container with a lid, or in a bottle, in the fridge.

raube

yoghurt starter

MAKES 1 LITRE (1¾ PINT)

You need 30 ml (2 tbsp) of the starter to 1 litre (1¼ pints) of milk. Bring milk gently to the boil – it is essential that it boils. Let it cool. The best way to judge the correct temperature is to carefully put your little finger in the milk. If you can keep it there just for as long as it takes to count to 10, it is the right temperature. Failure or success is determined by this traditional method. My sister-in-law, who is not Lebanese, could not get past the count of six when I first showed her how. The right temperature is 45 °C (113 °F). Remove the skin that forms on the surface of the milk. If by chance you forget the milk while it is cooling, it can be heated up again.

Put your starter in a porcelain bowl and stir until it has liquefied. Add a few spoons of the hot milk and stir again. Stir the starter mixture into the hot milk and pour into a container. Cover with a lid and wrap in a blanket. Leave it in a draught-free, warm place for at least 8 hours. The consistency should be thick and creamy. Refrigerate to prevent it becoming too sour. Eat the yoghurt as it is, use in sweet or savoury dishes, or add flavourings such as fruit.

yoghurt cream cheese

Add 5 ml (1 tsp) salt to 1 litre (1¼ pints) yoghurt. Put into a dampened muslin or cheesecloth bag, tie the corners and suspend over a bowl to drain. Over the kitchen sink is a good place, but do not do what my sister-in-law did – she tied it to a branch of a tree and promptly forgot about it. When she finally remembered and went to redeem it, the ants had beaten her to it!

When the mixture has drained, you will have a light, soft, cream cheese. This is delicious on toast with jam, or sprinkled with olive oil and paprika (or cayenne pepper if you like it strong) and eaten with bread.

Previous page: Yoghurt soup with dumplings (p. 40).

makaroon ib laban

yoghurt with rice & noodles

SERVES 6 – 8

125 g (4½ oz) flour
5 ml (1 tsp) salt
200 g (7 oz) long-grain rice

1.25 litres (2¼ pints) water, salted
15 ml (1 tbsp) vegetable oil
1.25 litres (2¼ pints) yoghurt
crushed garlic to taste
dried mint to taste

Make a stiff dough with flour, salt and enough water to bind. Roll out in long strips and cut into 2.5-cm (1-in) lengths. Cook the rice in salted water for about 15 minutes. Drop the noodles gently into the boiling rice and water. Allow to return to the boil, then add the vegetable oil and yoghurt and stir well. Simmer until rice and noodles are cooked. Before serving, add crushed garlic and dried mint.

yoghurt marinade

**MAKES ENOUGH FOR ABOUT 1 KG
(2¼ LB) CHICKEN PIECES**

1 clove garlic
salt and pepper
1 chicken stock cube

250 ml (8 fl oz) boiling water
60 ml (4 tbsp) lemon juice
15 ml (1 tbsp) vegetable oil
chilli sauce (optional)
chutney (optional)
250 – 500 ml (8 – 17 fl oz) yoghurt

In a large bowl, crush garlic with salt, add the chicken stock cube dissolved in the boiling water, lemon juice, pepper and oil. If desired, chilli sauce and a little chutney can be added to taste. Add beaten yoghurt. Coat chicken pieces well and leave in the marinade at room temperature or in the refrigerator for at least 1 hour, preferably overnight. Grill the chicken, basting with marinade, until the skin is brown and crisp and the juices run clear.

soups

SOUP OCCUPIES A large part in Lebanese culinary tradition, as it does with many nations. Here are a few of our specialities, all of which are meals in themselves.

rishta

noodles with lentils

This is a thick soup that can also be eaten cold. If possible, make your own noodles (see below), otherwise use bought ones. This dish is delicious served with plain yoghurt.

SERVES 6 – 8

450 g (1 lb) whole lentils (large brown ones
    if available)
1 – 2 onions, sliced
5 ml (1 tsp) ground coriander or some
    fresh coriander leaves

1 clove garlic, crushed (optional)
450 g (1 lb) noodles
black pepper
25 g (1 oz) butter (clarified, if possible)

Cover lentils with water, bring to the boil, cover pan and simmer for 50 minutes – 1 hour until soft, adding salt to taste. Drain. Fry onions in a little oil until soft. Add coriander and garlic, cook for a further 2 minutes. Add to lentils. If using homemade noodles, cook in boiling salted water for 5 minutes; bought noodles take 10 minutes. Drain and rinse, then add to lentils. Stir in butter.

noodles

125 g (4½ oz) sifted flour
5 ml (1 tsp) baking powder

pinch of salt
about 50 ml (2 fl oz) water

Sift together flour, baking powder and salt. Add enough water to mix to a smooth dough. Roll dough very thinly on a well-floured board and cut into thin strips. If you have a food processor, mix the ingredients in this. If you have a pasta machine, flour dough well and put pieces of dough through each roller until thin. Cut into strips. Cook as above and add lentils.

b'reesy

lamb & wheat soup

I do not know if you can term this a soup, but as it is always served in soup bowls and eaten with a spoon, we call it soup. It is so good its memory lingers for days. My mouth waters just thinking about it. It can be made with chicken or lamb. In both cases the meat should be boiled until it comes off the bone.

SERVES 8 – 10

450 g (1 lb) wholewheat berries or
    cracked wheat
450 g (1 lb) lamb (the neck and shoulder
    are especially good, but any part of the
    lamb will suffice) or 1 chicken (a not-too-
    young fowl is best)

salt and pepper
2.5 ml (½ tsp) cinnamon
1 ml (¼ tsp) allspice
15 – 30 ml (1 – 2 tbsp) ground cumin (this
    gives it the distinctive taste)

If using wheat berries, wash them and place in a container in which you can pound the wheat until the skin comes off. Let the wheat dry. Place the lamb or chicken in a large pot, cover with water, add salt and pepper and bring to the boil. Remove the scum and simmer until the meat can be removed easily from the bone (at least 2 hours for lamb, less for chicken).

In another pot, put the wheat and all the spices and add water to cover. Simmer until wheat is soft and bursts open. This should take about 3 hours.

Remove the meat from the bones and add the wheat, mashing both to the sides of the pot. The meat must look stringy and the mixture must not be too watery or mushy, but have a thick consistency. Check for seasoning.

Note: This soup sours very quickly in hot weather if left unrefrigerated for too long.

mahgluto qogool

soup of pulses

This soup is filling, nourishing and delicious. I usually add a chicken stock cube, but this is not traditional. This dish is equally good served cold the next day.

SERVE 8 – 10

100 g (4 oz) of each:
  chickpeas
  white butter beans
  pinto or red kidney beans

long-grain rice
lentils
cracked wheat
2 large onions, cut into rings
vegetable oil

Soak the chickpeas and beans overnight in plenty of water. Drain and rinse. Place soaked beans and chickpeas in a large pot with water and salt to taste. Bring to the boil and cook rapidly for 10 minutes, then reduce to a simmer, cover and cook for 1 hour. Add rice, lentils and cracked wheat and top up the pan with water. Bring back to the boil, cover and simmer for a further 15 mintues until the rice and lentils are cooked. Meanwhile, fry the onion rings in enough hot oil to cover, until very brown, but not burnt. Remove with a slotted spoon and stir into soup. Heat through for 5 minutes and serve.

shorbah bayd bi lamoun

soup with eggs & lemon

SERVES 8 – 10

carcass and giblets of 1 chicken
2 litres (3½ pints) water
salt and pepper
celery with leaves, chopped
1 leek, very finely chopped

3 cloves garlic, chopped
1 chicken stock cube
60 g (2½ oz) long-grain rice
2 eggs
juice of 2 lemons
chopped parsley or spring onions to garnish
  (optional)

Add chicken carcass and giblets to the water, add salt and pepper and bring to the boil, removing any scum. Add celery, leek and garlic. Simmer for 1 hour, then strain. Put stock back on stove and add chicken stock cube and rice (vermicelli or other fine noodles may be used instead of rice). Simmer until rice is tender. Lightly beat the eggs, then add the lemon juice and 5 ml (1 tsp) of the stock. Remove the stock from the heat and add the egg mixture, beating constantly until the stock thickens. For a sharper taste, add more lemon juice. Garnish with parsley or spring onions.

Soup of pulses (above).

shorbah bi kafte

meatball soup

Meatballs fried in butter make a very tasty dish on their own. Tomato purée can be added to this soup to give a richer flavour.

SERVES 6 – 8

2 marrow bones
250 g (9 oz) lamb neck or stewing beef
salt and pepper
1 cinnamon stick and 2.5 ml (½ tsp) cinnamon

450 g (1 lb) lamb or beef, minced
2.5 ml (½ tsp) allspice
25 g (1 oz) butter
200 g (7 oz) long-grain rice, washed
chopped parsley to garnish

Wash the marrow bones, crack them (so they exude more marrow) and place in a large pot with the meat. Add water to cover. Bring to the boil, removing scum. Add salt, pepper and cinnamon stick and simmer slowly for about 2 hours until you have a rich stock.

To prepare the meatballs, pulverize the minced meat to a paste (it can be processed in a food processor). Add salt, pepper, ground cinnamon and allspice and knead vigorously for a few minutes. Form the mixture into small balls and fry gently in the butter. When light in colour, add, together with the rice, to the soup. Simmer until the rice is cooked. Garnish with parsley.

adas b'sbaanegh (haamud)

lentil soup with spinach

SERVES 6 – 8

200 g (7 oz) red lentils, sifted through for
　　stones and washed
1.5 litres (2½ pints) water
2 onions, chopped
125 ml (4 fl oz) olive oil
1 kg (2¼ lb) spinach, well washed and

chopped (thick stalks removed), or
Chinese spinach may be used as is
1 – 2 cloves garlic, crushed with salt
1 stalk celery (optional)
small bunch coriander, washed and chopped
125 ml (4 fl oz) lemon juice
salt
5 ml (1 tsp) flour or cornflour (optional)

Place lentils in a large saucepan with water, bring to the boil, cover and simmer for 20 minutes. Brown the onions in the oil. Add spinach and garlic, mixing well. Cook slowly until spinach is soft, then add to lentils. Add rest of ingredients, except for flour. Let simmer for a while longer, adding more salt and lemon juice to taste.

If soup needs to be thickened, mix cornflour or flour with a little water. Add to soup and simmer, stirring, a few minutes longer until thickened.

Lentil soup with spinach (above).

shisbarak

yoghurt soup with dumplings

These dumplings can be made well in advance and frozen. Open-freeze them and then pack into polythene bags. This soup is also good with stuffed baby marrows, little balls of kibbi, small mince balls or any type of pasta. Garnish with fresh mint leaves.

SERVES 6 – 8

dumpling filling
450 g (1 lb) minced lamb
1 onion, chopped
salt and pepper
1 ml (¼ tsp) allspice
3 ml (¾ tsp) cinnamon
toasted pine nuts (optional)

dough
450 g (1 lb) flour
5 ml (1 tsp) salt
250 ml (8 fl oz) water
15 ml (1 tbsp) oil

Mix together lamb, onion, salt and pepper, allspice, cinnamon and pine nuts, if using. Make a firm dough with flour, salt, water and oil. Knead well, roll out until fairly thin and cut into approximately 5-cm (2-in) rounds. Put a little of the meat mixture in the centre of the dough, bring the edges up and pinch together. Bring the two corners together and twist to look like tortellini pasta. Dip in flour. To make these perfectly takes a little practice.

soup
1 – 2 litres (1¾ – 3½ pints) yoghurt
500 ml – 1 litre (17 fl oz – 1¾ pint) water
1 egg, beaten
15 ml (1 tbsp) flour or cornflour, mixed
   with a little water
100 g (4 oz) long-grain rice, washed
salt to taste
25 ml (1 tbsp) dried mint
3 – 4 cloves garlic, chopped
10 ml (2 tsp) butter
fresh mint leaves to garnish

Put yoghurt and water in a large saucepan. (For a tart taste, use less water or only yoghurt.) Beat well with rotary beaters until it has liquefied. Add egg and flour or cornflour. This stabilizes the yoghurt, as lengthy cooking causes cow's milk to curdle. Heat, stirring continuously with a wooden spoon until it boils. You must keep stirring as the milk can stick and burn. Once it boils, add the rice and salt to taste.

Drop in dumplings a few at a time, stirring continuously. Turn heat to low and cook gently for about 20 minutes. Grind the dried mint between palms of your hands and add to the soup. Meanwhile fry the garlic in butter. Add to soup. Garnish with fresh mint leaves.

rice

RICE IS ONE of the staple foods of the Lebanon. It is traditionally served as part of a main course and in stuffed vegetables as a mezze. It is put on the table with the hors d'œuvres, *mahshi* (stuffed dishes) and whatever else is being served, each person helping themselves to suit their individual taste.

Rice is always served with stew, bean stew and rice particularly go hand-in-hand. Try eating it with yoghurt. To stuff a chicken with rice, use the same basic filling as you do for stuffed vegetables (see p. 94), adding 60 g (2½ oz) slightly browned pine nuts. You can also add coarsely-chopped onions to the stuffing.

The traditional ritual of cooking rice is still adhered to even though today most brands are cleaned and parboiled.

To prepare rice in the traditional way, spread the rice on the table and remove all stones and foreign matter. Soak in boiling water for 20 – 30 minutes. Wash three to four times, rubbing the rice together with the palms of the hands. Whichever way you clean your rice, do soak it in boiling water first and rinse until the water runs clear, as this eliminates the starch. After the last wash put rice in a basin with lots of cold water and skim the top of the water to ensure that any remaining foreign bodies are removed. Pour into a strainer to drain or squeeze dry with hands.

riz

plain rice

Because the rice absorbs all of the cooking water in the following method, it is important to use the correct proportion of water to rice. The best way is to measure the volume of the rice and use the same amount of water. You can serve six to eight people with 600 g (1¼ lb) of rice.

SERVES 6 – 8

about 500 ml (17 fl oz) water
60 – 90 g (2½ – 3½ oz) butter (clarified,
  if possible)

600 g (1¼ lb) long-grain rice
5 ml (1 tsp) salt

Bring the water to the boil. Put butter (margarine or oil can be used, but are not traditional) in a large pot. Heat until the foam subsides, being careful not to burn (this is where clarified butter comes in handy and, incidentally, the taste is far superior to ordinary butter). Add well-drained rice, stir to coat well with the butter and cook for a minute or two, stirring all the time. Pour in boiling water to the same volume as the rice and add the salt. Boil for 2 minutes. Turn heat down very low, cover pot firmly and cook gently for 20 minutes. Turn off heat and let the rice stand for 10 minutes.

The rice should be fluffy and firm and each grain separate. If the rice is soft and mushy, too much water was added. To ensure the rice cooks very gently, you can place a heat diffuser under the pot if you like. A little lemon juice added to the cooking water helps keep rice white and separated.

m'jadrah

rice & lentils

In days gone by, this dish was generally referred to as 'dish of the poor'; food for the peasants, a meal for misers. The reason was that the lentils provided a good, yet inexpensive source of protein. Today it is enjoyed by all.

This is one of my favourite dishes. I generally prepare it on a Friday and not as frequently as in the past, because the whole, large brown lentils, which are delicious in this recipe, can sometimes be difficult to come by. *M'jadrah* is delightful eaten with yoghurt and fried fish. It can also be

Previous page: Rice with vermicelli (p. 43): Broad bean stew (p. 80).

served cold the next day with fried steak or leftover fish, or made into a salad by adding olive oil and lemon juice.

For an excellent garnish to this dish, fry 1 or 2 chopped onions in hot oil until they are very brown. The onions will caramelize and acquire a sweetish taste.

SERVES 6 – 8

400 g (14 oz) long-grain rice
100 g (4 oz) whole, large brown lentils

500 ml (17 fl oz) water
1.5 – 10 ml (⅓ – 2 tsp) salt
15 ml (1 tbsp) vegetable oil
3 – 4 large onions, sliced thinly into rings

Prepare rice as described on p. 41. Sift through the lentils for stones and foreign matter. Wash, put in a pot with the water and bring to the boil. Add salt. Cover and simmer for about 35 minutes until partly cooked, then add the rice, re-cover and simmer gently together for a further 15 minutes. In the meantime, heat the oil in a pan and brown the onion rings. Stir into the rice and lentils. This dish must not be dry, but the rice must not be mushy either – rather a little underdone than overcooked.

riz bi shirreeyeh

rice with vermicelli

SERVES 6 – 8

600 g (1¼ lb) long-grain rice
65 g (2½ oz) vermicelli
60 – 90 g (2¼ – 3½ oz) butter

about 500 ml (17 fl oz) boiling water
5 ml (1 tsp) salt
60 g (2¼ oz) toasted pine nuts or almonds
    (optional)

Prepare rice as described on p. 41. Break the vermicelli into small pieces. Melt the butter in a saucepan, add the vermicelli and brown well, stirring all the time. This can burn easily so do not leave the pot and do not stop stirring. When nicely browned, add the drained rice, coat well with the butter and cook for about 1 minute. Add boiling water and salt and stir. Boil vigorously for about 2 minutes, lower heat, cover tightly and cook slowly, undisturbed, for 20 minutes. Rice must be fluffy and firm and each grain separate.

Allow the rice to rest for about 10 minutes in the pot before serving.

Toasted pine nuts or almonds may be added to the rice. Fry whole or coarsely-chopped nuts in a little butter until just golden. Sprinkle over the top of the rice or spread evenly over the bottom of an oiled mould big enough to hold the rice. Press the rice tightly into the mould. Put a heated serving plate over the mould. Hold plate tightly and turn out onto plate.

makloubeh

rice layered with fish & cauliflower

SERVES 4 – 6

1 small cauliflower
30 ml (2 tbsp) vegetable oil

400 g (14 oz) cooked long-grain rice
450 g (1 lb) haddock, poached and flaked
salt and pepper
15 g (½ oz) butter

Separate the cauliflower into florets and fry in oil until golden and half cooked. Beginning with the rice, layer the ingredients in a baking dish (a glass one will show the layers to advantage), until all have been used, seasoning each layer. Dot with butter and bake in a hot oven (220 °C/ 425 °F/Gas 7) for 10 minutes. Serve with yoghurt.

riz ib haleeb

rice & milk

This dish always reminds me of my granny. Whenever she made rice and milk, she would tell me she was making it especially for me since I was so fond of it. It is delightful and the taste is luxuriously smooth. It was always given to someone who was not feeling well.

SERVES 4

200 g (7 oz) long-grain rice
250 ml (8 fl oz) water

500 ml (17 fl oz) milk
pinch of salt

Prepare the rice as described on p. 41. Boil together the rice, water, milk and salt. Cover and simmer gently until rice is cooked.

This dish can be made into a dessert by adding sugar to taste, 15 ml (1 tbsp) vanilla essence or rosewater; and thickening with cornflour. Decorate with cinnamon and chopped pistachio nuts.

fish & eggs

FISH USED TO play a big part in Lebanese homes as it was traditionally eaten on a
Friday and was served extensively over Easter. Today meat may be eaten on Fridays
and during Easter, with the exception of Good Friday. But old habits die hard and fish
is still a popular Friday dish.

samak maqli

fried fish

Serve with egg and lemon sauce or sesame sauce (see recipes below and on p. 49).

firm white fish

salt

oil for deep frying

parsley, onion rings or lemon wedges

to garnish

Wash and scale fish. If the fish is large, cut into slices or chunks. Salt well and leave to drain. Deep fry in hot oil ensuring the fish is completely covered – do not crowd fish when frying. Garnish with parsley, raw onion rings or lemon wedges.

bayd bi lamoun

egg & lemon sauce

Serve this sauce hot or cold on baked, grilled, fried or poached fish. To make fish stock use heads. Boil the heads in about 1 litre (1¾ pints) of water with lemon juice, chopped onion, garlic, a bay leaf, a celery stick if liked and a few black peppercorns for about 20 minutes. Strain.

MAKES 375 ml (13 fl oz)

375 ml (13 fl oz) fish stock

15 ml (1 tbsp) cornflour

3 egg yolks

juice of 1 lemon

salt and pepper

Put strained stock back onto stove and reheat. Mix cornflour with a little cold water and stir slowly into the stock, making sure the stock remains free of lumps. Keep stirring until sauce thickens, about 10 – 15 minutes. Beat the egg yolks and add the lemon juice, making sure the mixture is well stirred. Add about 15 ml (1 tbsp) of the hot sauce to the egg mixture, mix well and stir slowly into the stock. Season to taste. Keep stirring but do not let it boil. The sauce is ready when it is smooth, thick and creamy.

taratoor bi tahini

sesame sauce the Lebanese way

SERVES 4

2 – 3 cloves garlic
5 ml (1 tsp) salt
125 g (4½ oz) sesame paste (tahini)
juice of 1 – 2 lemons
30 ml (2 tbsp) chopped parsley
chopped parsley to garnish

Mash the garlic and salt in a bowl with a pestle
or wooden spoon. Stir in the sesame paste and
mix with enough water to make a white paste.
Add lemon juice and salt to taste and mix well
with a wooden spoon. The mixture should look
like mayonnaise. Stir in the parsley. Put cooked
fish into a baking dish. Pour the mixture over it, sprinkle with chopped parsley and bake for about
10 minutes at 160 °C/325 °F/Gas 3. You can also serve the sauce separately.

VARIATION

■ A mashed avocado mixed into this sauce transforms it into a lovely dip. Bread and almonds or
pine nuts can also be added.

2 slices of bread (crusts removed)   200 g (7 oz) almonds or pine nuts
water or milk, to soak bread

Soak bread in water or milk (I prefer the latter) and squeeze dry. Pound the nuts, then pound nuts
and bread together. Add the rest of the sesame sauce ingredients. Alternatively, simply process all
the ingredients together in a food processor.

kibbi samak

fish kibbi

This is a traditional Good Friday dish. The fish should be skinned and filleted. Wash the fish and sprinkle with salt, then drain in a colander. If possible, refrigerate for a few hours. All herbs should be thoroughly washed and spun in a lettuce spinner. I usually prepare the fish and herbs the day before as it is essential that they are very dry. Before using, I squeeze the herbs to make sure they are dry.

SERVES 6 – 8

1 kg (2¼ lb) white fish
1 large onion
1 – 2 bunches coriander
1 large bunch parsley (stalks removed)
30 ml (2 tbsp) fresh or 10 ml (2 tsp) dried
    mint

5 ml (1 tsp) grated orange or lemon rind
    (optional)
400 g (14 oz) cracked wheat, soaked in
    water at least 30 minutes
pinch allspice
7.5 – 10 ml (1½ – 2 tsp) ground cumin
2.5 ml (½ tsp) cinnamon
salt and pepper

Cut fish into large cubes. Divide into about four batches and purée the fish in a food processor with the onion and herbs. Some Lebanese cooks add grated orange or lemon rind at this stage. Put the mixture into a large mixing bowl. Squeeze out cracked wheat, a handful at a time, and add to the mixture. Add all the spices, salt and pepper to taste and knead together.

If using the filling (see recipe below), put half the mixture into a lightly-oiled baking tray. Cover with filling and then place the remaining mixture over the top. Smooth with wet hands and cut into diamond shapes (see p. 66). Pour over a little vegetable oil. Bake in a preheated oven at 180 °C/ 350 °F/Gas 4 for about 45 minutes. Remove from oven and drain off excess oil. Sprinkle with a little fresh olive or nut oil. The mixture can also be made into torpedo shapes to hold the filling. Shape the mixture around your index finger and put about 12 ml (2½ tsp) of the filling inside. Close the opening and deep-fry until golden. This dish is usually served cold with rice and lentils, a green salad and pickled turnips (see p. 13).

If not using the filling, simply spread the fish mixture in a baking tray and cook as above.

filling
The filling is not essential, but it is traditional.

3 – 4 onions, finely chopped
25 g (1 oz) pine nuts

30 ml (2 tbsp) vegetable oil
1 slice – 100 g (4 oz) white fish (optional)

Fry the onions and pine nuts in the oil until light brown. If using a slice of fish, chop finely and fry with the onions and pine nuts.

Clockwise from left: Fried fish (p. 48); Egg and lemon sauce (p. 48); Fish kibbi (above).

sumki b'tahini

baked fish in sesame sauce

SERVES 4

sesame sauce

1 – 2 cloves garlic, crushed with salt
125 g (4½ oz) sesame paste (tahini)
juice of 1 – 2 lemons or enough to make
    about 125 ml (4 fl oz)
1 onion, thinly sliced

1 whole hake, or fish of your choice
salt
olive oil
olives, parsley and lemon wedges or
    pomegranate seeds to garnish

To make the sauce, mix the garlic, sesame paste and lemon juice with enough water to form a mayonnaise consistency. Fry the onion in oil until transparent. Remove the onion with a slotted spoon and add to the sesame sauce.

Leave head on fish, but remove eyes. Wash and salt fish, leave to drain, then refrigerate for about 2 – 3 hours. Oil a baking dish big enough to hold the fish. Place the fish in the baking dish and pour just enough oil over it to make it glisten. Bake at 180 °C/350 °F/Gas 4 until just cooked. Pour the sauce over the fish and bake for a further 10 minutes.

Place a piece of olive over the eye. Garnish with parsley and lemon wedges or pomegranate seeds.

samak salamon kafta

salmon rissoles

SERVES 4

1 small tin salmon
salt and pepper
15 ml (1 tbsp) lemon juice
5 ml (1 tsp) parsley, chopped

2 eggs, beaten
50 g (2 oz) breadcrumbs or flour
breadcrumbs for coating
vegetable oil or butter
parsley to garnish

Remove salmon from the tin and remove all skin and bones. Flake and add salt, pepper, lemon juice, parsley, half the beaten eggs and sufficient breadcrumbs or flour to make a stiff mixture.

Form into rissoles, dip them in the remaining beaten egg and coat with breadcrumbs. Place on a greased baking tray with dabs of butter or oil on each rissole. Bake at 180 °C/350 °F/Gas 4 for 20 – 30 minutes. Garnish with parsley and serve with mashed potatoes and peas.

Baked fish in sesame sauce (above).

sayadiyya

fish with rice

SERVES 6

2 kg (4¼ lb) any fish of your choice,
    sliced into cutlets

salt and pepper

2 large onions, thinly sliced

250 ml (8 fl oz) olive oil

40 – 75 g (1½ – 3 oz) pine nuts

flour for dusting

15 ml (1 tbsp) ground cumin (optional)

1.25 litres (2¼ pints) boiling water

juice of 1 lemon

400 g (14 oz) long-grain rice, prepared as
    on p. 41

chopped parsley to garnish

Wash the fish, sprinkle with salt and leave to drain in a colander. If possible, cover and refrigerate for a few hours. Fry the onions in oil until golden or just softened. Remove with a slotted spoon. Fry the nuts until light brown, stirring all the time. Remove. Flour the fish and fry until golden, but not fully cooked. Remove, put onions back into pot, add the cumin, about 5 ml (1 tsp) salt and about 1.25 litres (2¼ pints) boiling water. Mix well and take out about 125 ml (4 fl oz) of this mixture to reserve for the sauce. Mix with the lemon juice and keep warm. Add rice to remaining boiling mixture, stir well and turn down to lowest heat. Cover and simmer until rice is almost cooked. Add fish and steam together until cooked.

Arrange rice on a platter. Garnish with pine nuts and parsley and serve with lemon sauce.

VARIATION

■ Do not fry the fish. After the onions have been browned, put them in a pot with the boiling water and simmer until very soft. Remove onions from heat, push the onions and water through a strainer and return to the pot. Remove some of the liquid, mix with the lemon juice and set aside for the sauce. Add the cumin and about 10 ml (2 tsp) salt. Place the floured fish in the pot. Bring to the boil, add the rice without stirring and simmer, covered, until cooked.

Turn out onto a round plate by putting the plate over the pot and turning the pot upside down. The fish should be moulded into the rice. You can brown some more onions to use as a garnish. Garnish further with a sprinkling of parsley and pine nuts. Either pour over the lemon sauce or serve separately.

Clockwise from left: Green bean salad (p. 110); Fish with rice (above); Sesame sauce (p. 49) with fried aubergines.

bayd bi gebna mehla

fried eggs with cheese

SERVES 1

1 egg
salt and pepper

1 slice haloumi, feta or other cheese
15 ml (1 tbsp) vegetable or olive oil
    or 15 g (½ oz) butter

Fry the cheese in oil or butter and, when it bubbles, crack the egg into it, being careful not to break the egg. Cook until the white sets. Sprinkle with salt and pepper and serve with Lebanese bread, flat bread or toast.

bayd bi towm

fried eggs with garlic & lemon

SERVES 6

15 g (½ oz) butter
6 eggs
5 ml (1 tsp) dried mint

2 cloves garlic, crushed
15 ml (1 tbsp) lemon juice
5 ml (1 tsp) salt

Mix the garlic with the lemon juice and salt. Heat the butter in a frying pan, add the garlic mixture and cook until garlic changes colour. Add eggs, being careful not to break them and fry until the whites are set. Crush the dried mint and sprinkle over the eggs.

bayd masloo'a

hard-boiled eggs with cumin

SERVES 6

salt
ground cumin

hard-boiled eggs, peeled

Cut the eggs in half or leave whole. In a small bowl, combine one part salt and two parts cumin. Sprinkle the mixture over the eggs or allow people to dip their own eggs into it.

Clockwise from top left: White broad bean salad (p. 109); Easter eggs (p. 60); Hard-boiled eggs with cumin (above); Black olives (p. 20).

bayd hamine

Easter eggs

This is an Easter favourite, when guests play the game of cracking one boiled egg against another to see who can crack the most eggs, keeping their own intact.

8 eggs
onion skins or food colouring
15 ml (1 tbsp) oil
30 ml (2 tbsp) ground coffee (optional)

Hard-boil the eggs in a pan of water containing lots of onion skins or food colouring and the oil, for 30 minutes. If you would like a a darker colour, add some ground coffee to the water. The result is a delightfully coloured egg.

bayd bi lagham i banadura

scrambled eggs with meat & tomatoes

SERVES 4 – 6

1 onion, chopped
25 g (1 oz) butter
500 g (1½ lb) cooked chopped meat or chicken, chicken livers or raw mince

4 – 5 tomatoes, peeled and chopped
salt and pepper
3 ml (¾ tsp) cinnamon
pinch each of allspice and ground cumin
1 garlic clove (optional)
6 eggs, lightly beaten

Soften the onion in the butter and add the meat. If raw, cook until well browned. If cooked, braise for a few minutes and then add the tomatoes, mixing well. Add salt, pepper, spices and garlic. Add the eggs and stir with a wooden spoon until cooked.

aegga

omelette

Almost anything can be used to fill an omelette – leftover meat, vegetables or prepared fillings.

SERVES 2 – 3

6 eggs
milk

filling of your choice
grated cheese

paprika and parsley or dried mint to garnish

Beat eggs, add a little milk and your chosen filling. Pour into a frying pan, set over a very low heat and cover. A stainless-steel pan is best for this purpose. When set, sprinkle lots of grated cheese over the top and garnish with paprika and parsley or dried mint.

aegga bi lagham

omelette with meat & tomatoes

Prepare as for scrambled eggs with meat and tomatoes (see p. 60), but let the eggs set instead of scrambling them.

aegga bi gibbis wa kousa

omelette with courgettes

This dish is usually served with yoghurt.

SERVES 3

15 g (½ oz) butter
1 onion, chopped
4 small courgettes, sliced

6 eggs
3 slices bread, crusts removed, soaked in
**   125 ml (4 fl oz) milk**
salt and pepper
chopped parsley and dried mint to garnish

Heat the butter and fry the onion until soft. Add courgettes and fry until light brown. Lightly beat the eggs and season to taste. Squeeze the milk from the bread and crumble into the eggs. Pour mixture over the courgettes and cook over a low heat until set. Garnish with chopped parsley and dried mint.

aegga bi karrat

leek omelette

SERVES 3

450 g (1 lb) leeks
25 g (1 oz) butter

juice of half a lemon
salt and pepper
6 eggs

Cut leeks into rounds. Wash well and drain. Heat the butter in a frying pan and gently cook the leeks until soft, adding a little water if necessary. Add lemon juice and salt and pepper to taste. Lightly beat the eggs, add to the pan and cook slowly until set.

VARIATION

■ If you have any spinach left over from a meal, shred it and use it in place of the leeks.

kibbi

KIBBI IS THE monarch of all meat dishes – it could almost be called the national dish of Lebanon. I recall when I was growing up that no Sunday lunch was complete without raw kibbi on the table. A stranger walking down our lane late on a Sunday morning would have been puzzled by the stamping noises coming from every house. It was made by the grandmothers and mothers sitting around their stone mortars, stamping the kibbi with their pestles. Believe me, they were heavy pestles and I am sure I would not manage to use one today as they did then.

Today kibbi is made in mincers or what we have come to call the 'kibbi machine' (a Moulinex patty maker). When it was discovered that this machine could cream the meat, it became so popular that the French manufacturers called one batch the 'kibbi maker' and had a picture of a plate of kibbi printed on the box. At one time these machines were very difficult to come by, as the Lebanese community snatched them up as soon as they came into the country. A food processor may also be used.

kibbi nay

raw kibbi & basic kibbi mixture

A Lebanese proverb:
Kul balad zayy wakul sa jarra layy.
Every town has its customs and every tree has its shade.

Each household has its own individual method for making this speciality which is eaten raw like steak tartare. If you are eating kibbi for the first time, you will be none the wiser, but connoisseurs will know the exact ingredients and proportions used. This basic mixture is used when making baked or fried kibbi.

SERVES 6 – 8

1 leg or shoulder of lamb weighing 2 kg (4¾ lb)
salt
cracked wheat – 200 g (7 oz) to each 450 g
   (1 lb) of meat
1 onion
1 green pepper (optional)

a few sprigs fresh or dried mint
parsley (optional)
1 hot chilli (optional)
1 ml (¼ tsp) allspice
2.5 ml (½ tsp) cinnamon
10 – 12 ml (2 – 3 tsp) ground cumin
lamb tail fat (if available)
mint and spring onions for garnish

Cut meat off the bone, discarding all the gristle, fat and sinew. Some meat has more sinew than others and this is definitely the worst part of preparing kibbi. Some cooks say it is not necessary to cut it all off when mincing with the kibbi machine, but I disagree. Regardless of the method for creaming the meat, the sinew should be removed, as the finished appearance is so much better. (Keep the bones, shanks and bits and pieces for gravy, stew and soup.)

Cube the meat and weigh it. Salt the cubes and, if possible, refrigerate for a few hours or overnight. This is not absolutely necessary, but it does enhance the flavour. Soak the cracked wheat in plenty of water for at least half an hour.

If you are mincing the meat, then add alternate pieces of onion to the mincer, as well as the green pepper, mint, parsley and chilli, if using. Mince three or four times until the mixture is very creamy. (If you like, put some of the cracked wheat through with the mixture after the last mincing. This is a matter of preference.)

If you are using a kibbi machine or food processor, put in small quantities of meat, together with a little of the onion, green pepper, mint, parsley and chilli. Hold the lid down with the machine running for the count of 10, lift the lid to the count of 10 then repeat the process. The meat must be creamy, but not mushy. Remove, adding more until all the meat is minced. Put the mixture into a large basin. I find the stainless-steel ones best.

Squeeze the cracked wheat with your hands and add to mixture. Add the balance of ingredients to the mixture. Mix well and taste for seasoning. Have iced water handy. Dip your hands in the iced water and knead with fists, turning meat over and kneading further, as though you are mixing

Previous page: Aubergines with sesame paste (p.107); Baked kibbi (p. 66).

bread dough. Keep dipping your hands in iced water. This keeps the meat smooth and helps to cream it.

To serve kibbi, arrange on a platter, rubbing iced water over the top of the kibbi for a shiny, smooth finish. Decorate the edges with sprigs of mint or spring onions. My grandmother always made the sign of the cross in the centre of the kibbi and this tradition is still maintained by all the members of the family. An oil sauce (see p. 66) is then dribbled over individual servings and the kibbi is eaten with bread. The bread is torn off and held between the thumb and first two fingers of the hand and then used to scoop up the kibbi.

kibbi arnabiyye

kibbi balls with chickpeas & sesame sauce

For this dish use up all of your leftover meat and bones from a leg of lamb.

SERVES 6 – 8

1 quantity kibbi mixture (see pp. 64–5)
leftover lamb and bones
1 beef shin bone (optional)
200 g (7 oz) chickpeas, soaked overnight
2 large onions, sliced into thin rings
30 ml (2 tbsp) olive oil, butter or clarified
    butter
40 g (1½ oz) sesame paste (tahini)
juice of 1 lemon

Prepare kibbi. Wet your hands and break off small balls of the mixture. Place meat and bones in a large pot with enough water to cover. Bring to the boil and skim off the scum that forms. Drain and rinse chickpeas. When there is no longer a trace of scum, add chickpeas. Simmer for about 1½ hours until chickpeas are very soft and meat is tender. Remove the meat, cut it off the bones and return to the pot. Fry onions in oil, clarified butter or plain butter until well browned, being careful not to burn. Add to the pot. Mix well and allow to simmer for 5 – 10 minutes. Whilst this is simmering, cream sesame paste with the juice of a lemon and a little water. Add to pot, stirring all the time. Add the kibbi balls and simmer for 5 – 10 minutes. Serve in soup bowls with rice.

kibbit batatah b'saneh

potato kibbi

This dish can be served hot or cold with a salad.

SERVES 6

6 medium potatoes, scrubbed
salt and pepper
300 g (11 oz) cracked wheat, soaked in
    water for 30 minutes
1 onion, thinly sliced
100 g (4 oz) chopped parsley
2.5 ml (½ tsp) cinnamon
1 ml (⅛ tsp) allspice
15 ml (1 tbsp) dried mint
60 g (2¼ oz) flour (optional)
125 ml (4 fl oz) olive oil

Cook potatoes in their skins in salted water until soft. Peel and mash. Squeeze out water from cracked wheat. Add to potatoes with onion, parsley, spices, mint and plenty of salt and pepper. Moisten hands with water and knead mixture well. If mixture is too soft, add flour. Keep kneading until mixture is firm. Press mixture into a baking tray and cut into diamond shapes as described in recipe for baked kibbi (see p. 66). Pour over oil and bake in a hot oven at 180 °C/350 °F/Gas 4 for about 40 minutes until golden.

meat & poultry

MEAT IS USED in many Lebanese dishes, although other ingredients are so plentiful and recipes so versatile that if there was a shortage of meat one could get by without it. But to do without the wonderful grilled meat and tasty, nourishing stews would be to miss out on some truly delicious meals. Of all the meats, lamb is most frequently used.

lagham mashwi

grilled meat

My mouth waters at the mere mention of this dish. When I was a little girl, the meat was grilled over wood shavings and other bits and pieces brought from the picture-framing factory. To this day, I feel that meat grilled over wood is far superior to any other. On many a winter's evening, when the fire had burned low in the lounge, someone would suggest making grilled meat and the evening was reborn. Try it and you will find that, in addition to summer guests, you will have winter guests popping in frequently.

Most people are familiar with grilling steaks and chops, so I will only give the method for grilling with skewers. Cubed steak can be used, but lamb or mutton is traditional.

Cut bite-sized pieces from the leg or shoulder (shoulder meat is sweeter). Season with salt and pepper and thread onto skewers. Grill over a very low fire for maximum flavour and succulence. Have Lebanese bread on hand to wrap around the meat, and to soak up the juices. This can only be enjoyed to the full by eating with your fingers and, believe me, this is food 'fit for the gods'.

Take care not to overcook the meat – it should take about 7 – 10 minutes. The outside must be crisp and a rich brown. The inside must be juicy and a little pink, unless you prefer it otherwise. You may want to grill other foods on the skewers. Alternate with the meat whatever you have handy, such as quartered tomatoes, pieces of onion, green pepper, mushroom, etc.

marinade

If you want a marinade for a simple barbecue, try the following:

MAKES ENOUGH FOR 1 KG (2¼ LB) OF MEAT

2 – 3 cloves garlic
salt and pepper
125 ml (4 fl oz) olive oil

2 onions, crushed to extract the juice
juice of 1 lemon
1 bay leaf, crushed
2.5 ml (½ tsp) cinnamon
5 ml (1 tsp) ground cumin (optional)
pulp of 2 tomatoes (optional)

Crush the garlic with salt and stir in the balance of ingredients, mixing well. Coat the meat and marinate for at least 3 hours at room temperature, making sure that the meat is well covered. The meat can be marinated for a few hours and then frozen, or can be left in the marinade in the refrigerator for as long as a week.

A leg of lamb or mutton marinated in this mixture, then roasted on a rôtisserie or in a cooking bag or foil in the oven, is delicious.

VARIATION

■ Whisk together 300 ml (½ pint) plain yoghurt and the juice of a lemon. Add yoghurt mixture to the marinade in the previous recipe and marinate as before. Chicken is also excellent marinated in this mixture.

Previous page: Duck with orange juice (p. 85). This page: Grilled meat (see above).

gham'mee or krush mahshi

stuffed tripe

SERVES 4 – 6

200 g (7 oz) long-grain rice

750 g (1¾ lb) coarsely-ground lamb or beef
   or a mixture

1 ml (¼ tsp) allspice

2.5 ml (½ tsp) cinnamon

2 ml (¼ tsp) saffron (optional)

30 ml (2 tbsp) finely chopped chickpeas (soak
   overnight, drain and rinse first)

3 large onions (2 cubed and 1 quartered)

salt and pepper

25 g (1 oz) butter, melted

1.5 kg (3¼ lb) tripe (wash thoroughly and
   remove fat)

1 pigs' trotter (well scraped and cleaned)

1 stick cinnamon

Prepare the rice as described on p. 41. Mix together the rice, meat, spices, chickpeas, cubed onions, salt and pepper and melted butter to make a stuffing. Cut the tripe into serving squares and salt both sides. Fold each piece in half and stitch three sides. Fill with stuffing and stitch the opening. Place tripe and trotters in a large pot with enough water to cover. The trotters will enhance the flavour of the dish tremendously. Also add the cinnamon stick, the quartered onion and salt and pepper to taste. Bring to the boil and keep skimming off the scum until clear. Lower heat and simmer for 3 – 4 hours. Unstitch the tripe, keeping the stuffing inside. Arrange on a platter and serve with boiled parsley potatoes. You may serve the broth separately or keep it to make a soup.

d'megh

brains

SERVES 4 – 6

lamb's brains
white wine vinegar
125 ml (4 fl oz) water
45 ml (3 tbsp) vegetable oil

5 ml (1 tsp) ground cumin (optional)
salt and pepper
juice of ½ – 1 lemon
2 – 3 cloves garlic, crushed
turmeric for colour (optional)
parsley to garnish

Soak brains in water with a little vinegar for about 1 hour. Wash well and remove all membranes. Put water into a pot, add oil, cumin, salt, pepper, lemon juice and garlic and bring to the boil. Turn heat to low, add brains and simmer very gently for about 10 minutes. If you want colour, add turmeric to the water. Remove brains carefully so as not to break them. Put on a platter and pour over the juices left in the pot. Garnish with parsley.

d'megh bi saniyyeh

roasted brains

SERVES 4 – 6

450 g (1 lb) brains (any type)
white wine vinegar

vegetable oil
salt and pepper
1 egg

Soak, wash and remove membranes as per directions above. Place in a roasting tin. Pour over enough oil to coat the brains. Season to taste. Bake for 40 minutes in a moderate oven at 180 °C/ 350 °F/Gas 4. Beat egg until frothy and pour over the brains. Bake for a further 10 minutes. Serve with a green salad.

kelwaewi

kidneys

SERVES 4 – 6

600 g (1¼ lb) kidneys
25 g (1 oz) butter

salt and pepper
juice of 1 large lemon
chopped parsley to garnish

Remove skin and membrane from kidneys and halve them. Melt butter and fry kidneys gently for a few minutes until colour changes. Season to taste and sprinkle with lemon juice. Garnish with parsley.

klewe bi banadura

kidneys with tomatoes

SERVES 4 – 6

600 g (1¼ lb) kidneys
1 onion, chopped
1 clove garlic, crushed

25 g (1 oz) butter
30 ml (2 tbsp) tomato purée
4 tomatoes, skinned and sliced
salt and pepper

Prepare kidneys as described on p. 75. Fry chopped onion and garlic in butter, then add kidneys. Fry for 2 – 3 minutes. Mix the tomato purée with a little water and add to kidneys, together with tomatoes and salt and pepper. Simmer gently for about 15 minutes.

mikharat (kasbi - kibda)

chopped liver

The two-knife method is not required for chopping liver.

SERVES 4 – 6

600 g (1¼ lb) calf's or lamb's liver
salt and pepper
25 g (1 oz) butter
1 large onion, sliced

3 cloves garlic
5 ml (1 tsp) flour
5 ml (1 tsp) dried mint, crushed
125 ml (4 fl oz) white wine vinegar
about 125 ml (4 fl oz) water

Slice liver into strips, sprinkle with salt and pepper. Heat butter and fry onions until golden. Add the garlic crushed with salt, flour and mint. Add the vinegar, water and salt and pepper to taste. Slowly bring to the boil, stirring all the time. Cook, stirring, for about 5 minutes. Add liver and, if necessary, more water to cover. Simmer gently for a further 5 minutes.

kroueen bi hoummus

trotters with chickpeas

SERVES 4 – 6

225 g (8 oz) chickpeas, soaked overnight

salt and pepper
8 lamb's trotters
hard-boiled eggs to garnish

Drain and rinse chickpeas. Wash trotters thoroughly, scraping between the folds. Place trotters in a large saucepan, cover with water and bring to the boil, removing the scum that forms. Add seasoning and chickpeas. Turn heat down to very low and simmer for about 4 hours or pressure-cook for 1 hour. Remove meat and chickpeas with a slotted spoon and arrange on a serving platter. Garnish with hard-boiled eggs.

Potatoes, rice or pasta can be used in place of chickpeas, in which case they are added about 20 – 30 minutes before the end of the cooking time. Butter beans may also replace the chickpeas. Chillies or cayenne pepper may be used to create a spicy dish. To make a richer dish, fry onions with the trotters and add a chicken stock cube for extra flavour.

stews

L EBANESE STEWS ARE spicy, aromatic, mouthwatering to look at and delicious to eat. No matter how replete I feel when visiting relatives, if green bean stew with lamb is being served, I am unable to resist. It must be served with rice made with or without vermicelli. The two complement each other.

The basic preparation of the meat is the same for all stews. In the past, clarified mutton or lamb fat, particularly from the tail, was used for braising. For health reasons, this practice is no longer widespread.

This brings to mind an incident involving my daughter when she was about 18 months old and we were visiting an aunt of mine. As my daughter was very quiet, I went to investigate and found her in the scullery sitting in a pot of clarified fat. She was covered in fat from head to toe and was having a wonderful time. It took days to get the gooey mess out of her hair and to clean the floor and walls, and all the fat had to be thrown away.

yaghni bi loobyeh

green bean stew with lamb

SERVES 6

1 kg (2¼ lb) fresh green beans (stringless)

1 kg (2¼ lb) lamb (ribs or shoulder)

2 onions, finely chopped or thinly sliced

15 ml (1 tbsp) vegetable oil butter (if required)

2 – 3 tomatoes, skinned and chopped or grated

2.5 ml (½ tsp) cinnamon

1 ml (⅕ tsp) allspice

15 ml (1 tbsp) tomato purée

2.5 ml (½ tsp) grated nutmeg (optional)

1 – 2 cloves garlic, crushed

salt and pepper

1 chicken or beef stock cube (optional)

lemon juice (optional)

Wash, top and tail the beans and break in half if necessary. There are two schools of thought as to whether one should braise the onions or the meat first. In our family, we braise the meat first.

Cube the meat, place in a thick-bottomed pot and braise in its own fat until brown, stirring constantly. Add beans and fry together. Add onions and a little oil or butter, if required. Cook until onions are soft. Add tomatoes and the remaining ingredients. (I add a chicken or beef stock cube at this stage too. This is optional.) Stir well and let simmer on lowest heat, undisturbed for about 1 hour. Check for tenderness and add water if required. Some lemon juice can be added, if desired.

Okra stew (p. 80).

yaghni bisella

pea stew

Prepare as for green bean stew with lamb (see p. 79), but replace the beans with 900 g (2 lb) fresh or frozen peas and add them after the tomatoes and water. If using frozen peas (which take about 8 minutes to cook), cook the meat until it is almost done before adding peas . If using tinned peas, add at the end of cooking time. Pour in the water from the tin as well, as this has all the goodness.

yaghni fasoulya

broad or butter bean stew

Prepare as for pea stew (above), replacing the peas with 900 g (2 lb) dried broad or butter beans, soaked overnight, drained and rinsed. Add more garlic as this enhances the dish. Precook the beans so the meat does not overcook and add the cooking water from the beans to the stew. Tinned beans are a useful standby. Add at the end of cooking.

yaghni bamiey

okra stew

Prepare as for green bean stew with lamb (see p. 79), replacing the beans with 1 kg (2¼ lb) fresh okra or 1 large tin. If using fresh okra, wash and cut off the stems. Be careful not to overcook the stew, as the okra can become mushy.

If using tinned okra, do not braise with the meat and onions, but add about 10 minutes before the end of cooking time.

yaghni l'orse

potato stew

Prepare as for green bean stew with lamb (see p. 79), substituting 900 g (2 lb) quartered potatoes for the green beans.

poultry

THE TRADITIONAL METHOD of preparing poultry is meticulous and thorough. In the early days, poultry was usually slaughtered at home or purchased with the feathers and intestines intact. Today's sophisticated machinery has eliminated all this 'off-putting' work, but while the chickens are usually de-feathered, you may still find hairs which must be singed off. This can be done over a gas flame or a candle.

kafta

chicken balls

This is a very good way of using up leftover chicken. If, like me, you are not fond of the breast, this is a useful way of using this portion.

SERVES 6

450 g (1 lb) boneless cooked chicken
1 thick slice white bread, soaked in milk
15 g (½ oz) pistachio nuts, pine nuts
   or almonds
15 ml (1 tbsp) vegetable oil

juice of 1 lemon
salt and pepper
15 ml (1 tbsp) chopped parsley
2.5 ml (½ tsp) dried mint (optional)
flour
oil for frying

Mince chicken. Squeeze the soaked bread in the palms of your hands and add to chicken. Finely chop the nuts. If using pine nuts or almonds, fry them lightly first. Add to the chicken mixture with the oil, lemon juice, salt, pepper and parsley. Dried mint can be added as well. Combine well, kneading the mixture. Shape into little balls. If serving as an hors d'œuvre, shape into bite-sized balls. Roll the balls in flour and fry in oil. Serve hot or cold.

Instead of frying the balls, you can add them to a stew or soup and simmer until heated through.

djegh m'hammara

fried chicken

Season chicken portions with salt and pepper, and coat with flour, if liked. Deep-fry in hot oil or a mixture of butter and oil. If served hot, a butter and oil mixture is much nicer.

djegh fil forn mahshi

roast chicken with stuffing

SERVES 6

50 g (2 oz) butter

1 onion, finely chopped

250 g (9 oz) chicken giblets (liver, heart and gizzard), coarsely chopped or mince

15 – 25 g (½ – 1 oz) pine nuts or almonds, blanched and chopped

150 g (5 oz) long-grain rice

450 ml (¾ pint) boiling water

salt

2 – 3 cloves garlic (optional)

60 ml (4 tbsp) plain yoghurt

1 large chicken

Melt butter, let foam subside and gently fry the chopped onion until soft, but not brown (about 5 minutes). Add giblets or mince and fry for a further 2 – 3 minutes until there is no trace of pink in the meat. Add pine nuts or almonds and fry until golden, being careful as they burn easily. Add washed and drained rice and stir well until rice glistens with butter.

Add boiling water and salt. Turn heat to lowest setting and simmer until all the liquid has evaporated – about 20 minutes. Cool.

Stuff prepared, cleaned chicken with cooled mixture. Secure the neck skin at the back and truss securely. If using garlic, crush it with salt, add yoghurt and pour some of the mixture over the chicken. Place the chicken in a shallow roasting tin and roast at 180 °C/350 °F/Gas 4, basting with the rest of the yoghurt mixture, until tender – about 90 minutes. Test with a skewer: the juices that run out must be clear or pale yellow – if still showing pink, roast longer. If there is any leftover stuffing, reheat and serve with the chicken.

VARIATION

■ Use the same basic filling as the one given for vegetables (see p. 94), adding fried pine nuts. Stuff the chicken then cover with water and simmer for about 45 minutes, removing any scum that forms. When the chicken is almost done, remove to a roasting pan, drizzle some melted butter over it and roast in the oven at 180 °C/350 °F/Gas 4 for about 20 minutes, until the chicken is golden in colour.

Fried chicken (p. 82); Hoummus (p. 105); boiled potatoes.

djegh mishwi

grilled chicken

This is always a firm favourite. For variation, adding plain yoghurt to the marinade is delicious.

SERVES 4 – 6

1 chicken, cut into serving pieces
salt and pepper

marinade
2 – 3 cloves garlic
10 ml (2 tsp) salt

1 onion, finely chopped
juice of 1 – 2 lemons
30 – 45 ml (2 – 3 tbsp) oil
cayenne pepper or crushed chilli
black pepper
1 chicken stock cube dissolved in 125 ml
   (4 fl oz) boiling water

Season the chicken with salt and pepper. In an enamel, stainless-steel, plastic or glass dish, crush the garlic with the salt until it is creamy. Add the rest of the ingredients and mix well. Add the chicken pieces and coat with the marinade – this is best done with your hands. Make sure each piece is well covered and refrigerate for at least 2 – 3 hours, preferably overnight. Grill and, when almost done, baste with leftover marinade.

djegh b'hoummus ou riz b'sahgriah

chicken with chickpeas, vermicelli & rice

This dish is prepared in sections. A whole large chicken is usually used, either cut up before cooking or stripped off the bone before serving. I prefer to use a whole chicken and joint it before cooking, as it has more flavour than bought chicken pieces. Wash the chicken, salt and leave to drain.

SERVES 12

1 chicken, jointed

2 onions, thinly sliced

1 clove garlic, crushed with salt

3 litres (5¼ pints) water

30 ml (2 tbsp) vegetable oil

1 cinnamon stick

125 g (4½ oz) chickpeas, soaked in water overnight

75 g (3 oz) slivered almonds or pine nuts

225 g (8 oz) melted butter (clarified if possible) or a mixture of butter and oil

600 g (1¼ lb) minced lamb or beef topside or a mixture (the meat should not be too finely minced)

2.5 ml (½ tsp) cinnamon

1 ml (⅕ tsp) allspice

salt and pepper

50 g (2 oz) broken-up vermicelli

200 g (7 oz) rice, prepared as on p. 41

Fry the chicken, half the onions and the crushed garlic in the oil until golden. Add about 2 litres (3½ pints) water and the cinnamon stick and simmer until tender. Remove chicken pieces and keep warm. Retain the chicken stock.

Meanwhile, drain and rinse the chickpeas and boil in 1 litre (1¾ pints) water for about 1 hour until tender. Brown the nuts in most of the butter, stirring all the time as they burn easily. Remove the nuts with a slotted spoon and set aside. Brown the minced meat in the butter, adding more butter if necessary. Sauté meat, breaking up any lumps against the side of the pot. Add remaining onions and braise until soft. Add cinnamon, allspice and salt and pepper to taste. Cook for about 15 - 20 minutes. Set aside.

In a large pot, sauté the vermicelli in the remaining butter, stirring all the time, as this also burns easily. Add drained rice and mix together until the vermicelli and rice are well coated with the butter. Add 1.5 litres (2½ pints) boiling broth from chicken. Stir well and add the meat and onion and chickpeas. Mix well, turn heat to low, cover and simmer until rice is cooked and liquid absorbed (about 20 minutes). Turn off heat and leave for 10 minutes.

Transfer rice and meat to a platter, and put the chicken pieces on top. Garnish with the nuts. This meal is well worth the trouble and makes a great party dish.

bata bi lamoun

duck with orange juice

SERVES 4

1 medium-sized duck (2.2 – 3 kg/5 – 6½ lb)
salt and pepper
40 g (1½ oz) butter
1 large onion, thinly sliced

25 g (1 oz) flour
juice of 1 sweet orange
juice of 1 bitter Seville orange (use 2 sweet oranges if bitter are unavailable)
1 bay leaf (optional)

Wash duck, removing any pin feathers. Season with salt and pepper and leave in a colander to drain. Brown duck in the butter. Remove. Cook the onion until transparent, add flour and cook, stirring all the time, for about 1 minute. Add 15 ml (1 tbsp) water and stir well. Put the duck back in the pot and add orange juices and salt to taste. Adding a bay leaf will improve the flavour. Cover and simmer for about 1 hour, adding more water if necessary. Remove duck, joint, return to pot and simmer until tender and juices absorbed.

habash mihshi

stuffed turkey

SERVES 12

1 turkey weighing 5 kg (11 lb)
salt
500 ml (17 fl oz) plain yoghurt

stuffing

40 g (1½ oz) butter (clarified if possible) or
45 ml (3 tbsp) vegetable oil
450 g (1 lb) coarsely minced lamb or a
    mixture of lamb, veal and beef topside
    (the mince must not be too fine, it should
    be chopped using the two-knife method
    described on p. 73, or ask a butcher to
    mince coarsely)

200 g (7 oz) long-grain rice (prepared as
    on p. 41)
100 g (4 oz) pine nuts, slivered almonds or
    chopped macadamia nuts
1.5 ml (¼ tsp) allspice
2.5 ml (½ tsp) cinnamon
5 ml (1 tsp) ground cumin
salt and pepper
a little melted butter or clarified butter
500 ml (17 fl oz) plain yoghurt

Mix all the stuffing ingredients together.

Remove turkey's neck bone, which can be used to make a sauce. Clean turkey inside, ensuring that all fat and giblets are removed. Stuff turkey with the rice stuffing and cover with the neck skin. Sew up opening. Place turkey in a large pot with water to cover, adding salt. Bring to the boil and remove scum from the surface. Lower heat and simmer slowly until tender, about 2 – 2½ hours. Transfer turkey to tin, pour yoghurt over and brown in a hot oven at 200 °C/400 °F/Gas 6.

VARIATIONS

■ Wrap the turkey in foil or place in an oven roasting bag and roast at 180 °C/350 °F/Gas 4 for 25 minutes per 450 g (1 lb), plus an additional 25 minutes. Remove the turkey when almost done, pour over the yoghurt and return to oven until browned.

■ Prepare as above and cook in a barbecue kettle according to manufacturer's instructions. This is a very good way to cook turkey. Baste with yoghurt towards the end of cooking time.

vegetables & salads

VEGETABLES ARE NOT just plain boiled affairs to the Lebanese. They play a very important part in many meals, and it is often difficult to differentiate between a meat course and a vegetable dish, because vegetables frequently play the bigger part. I have endeavoured to divide them into separate sections, dealing with the meatiest stews in the previous chapter.

Note that the number of servings given with each recipe is only a guide, as portion size depends on the type of meal – if you are serving a selection of mezze, then guests will want only a small amount of each dish.

Remember to boil vegetables in as little water as possible and keep the cooking water to add to soups, stews or gravies.

loobyea kho'dar

green beans

SERVES 4

450 g (1 lb) fresh green beans
1 onion, chopped
1 clove garlic, crushed
30 ml (2 tbsp) vegetable oil

5 ml (1 tsp) tomato purée
2 large tomatoes, skinned and chopped
2.5 ml (½ tsp) cinnamon
1 ml (¼ tsp) allspice
salt and pepper

Top and tail beans. If very long, break into halves or quarters. Sauté onion and garlic in oil until soft and transparent. Add tomato purée and beans, stir to coat well and cook for a few minutes. Add tomatoes, spices, salt, pepper and water to cover. Simmer slowly until soft, but not mushy. This dish can be served hot or cold.

koraat bi burghal

leeks with cracked wheat

This is a family favourite. When my son and his wife moved away, one of his phone calls home to me was a plea to tell his wife how to make this dish.

SERVES 6 – 8

30 ml (2 tbsp) cracked wheat
900 g (2 lb) leeks
30 ml (2 tbsp) oil
1 onion, sliced
salt and pepper

Soak the cracked wheat in plenty of water for at least 30 minutes. Drain and squeeze dry. Slice leeks into thin rounds, discarding tough ends. Wash thoroughly and drain. Heat oil in a saucepan and sauté the onion until soft. Add leeks and cook for a few minutes. Add salt and pepper and cracked wheat. Cook gently to warm through, adding a little water if necessary. Serve hot or cold.

VARIATION
■ Cabbage can be used in place of leeks, in which case chop or slice cabbage and proceed as above.

bamja

okra (ladies' fingers)

SERVES 4

600 g (1¼ lb) okra, fresh or tinned

2 large onions, sliced

3 cloves garlic, roughly chopped

30 ml (2 tbsp) vegetable oil

3 – 4 tomatoes, skinned and chopped or
    grated

2.5 ml (½ tsp) cinnamon

2.5 ml (½ tsp) allspice

salt and pepper

15 ml (1 tbsp) lemon juice

If using fresh okra, cut off stems, then wash and drain well. Fry the onions and garlic in oil until soft. Add okra and fry until pliable. Add tomatoes and spices and season to taste. Simmer for about 1 hour without disturbing the okra, if possible, until it is very soft, but not broken. Tinned okra takes less time to cook.

Add the lemon juice and simmer a while longer. Place a plate over the top of the pot and turn the okra out carefully; it should come out as though moulded. This dish can be served cold.

ba'ta'tis bi hoummus

potatoes with chickpeas

SERVES 6 – 8

250 g (9 oz) chickpeas, soaked overnight

2 large onions, sliced

30 ml (2 tbsp) vegetable oil

2 cloves garlic

1 kg (2¼ lb) potatoes, thinly sliced

450 g (1 lb) tomatoes, skinned and chopped
    or grated

30 ml (2 tbsp) tomato purée

salt and pepper

Drain and rinse the chickpeas, place in a large saucepan, cover with water and bring to the boil. Cover the pan and simmer for 40 minutes. Meanwhile, fry onions in the oil for 15 minutes until soft and golden. Add whole garlic cloves, drained chickpeas and add potatoes, stir well and cook for a few minutes. Add tomatoes, tomato purée and sufficient water to cover. Season. Bring to the boil, cover and simmer for 20 – 25 minutes until tender. This dish is delicious served hot or cold.

AUBERGINES CAME TO the Middle East from India more than 150 years ago. In this region, where they are called the 'poor man's caviare' or 'poor man's meat', it is said that there are more than 120 ways of cooking them. In any case they are loved equally by peasant and prince. Remember when buying aubergines to choose firm fruit with smooth, unshrivelled skin. A heavy aubergine has fewer seeds.

moussaka tabek batenghen

layered baked aubergines

This is a very controversial dish as the Greeks, the Yugoslavs, the Lebanese and the Russians all claim it as theirs. The word *moussaka* is Arabic. But to whomever it may belong, and in all its different guises, it is delicious and a wonderful party dish. This version is not typically Lebanese – it came originally from an Italian friend who gave the recipe to my cousin. She in turn passed it on to me and the rest of our family and friends. It is never fails to please and is hailed by all and sundry, with the exception of my husband who, of all things, is allergic to aubergines.

This dish freezes very well, so make a double quantity to compensate for the work put into it. Make your favourite bolognaise sauce. (Incidentally, lasagne can be made this way by substituting the pasta for the aubergines.) Boil the pasta first in salted water and then rinse under the cold tap.

SERVES 4 – 6

750 g (1¾ lb) bolognaise or meat sauce
3 – 4 large aubergines
salt
vegetable oil for frying
600 ml (1 pint) béchamel sauce (see opposite)
grated cheese

Have your meat sauce ready. Make a classic bolognaise sauce, using minced lamb or beef, or add mushrooms, cream and wine to tomato gravy. You can also use chopped chicken.

Peel aubergines thinly or if you prefer leave the skin on (this looks attractive if you bake them in a glass dish). Slice them from top to bottom in fairly thick slices, salt and leave for about 30 minutes to drain. Fry the slices lightly in oil, then drain on paper towels.

béchamel sauce

600 ml (1 pint) milk	salt and pepper
50 g (2 oz) butter	good pinch nutmeg
60 g (2½ oz) flour	1 egg, beaten (optional)

Boil the milk. In another pot melt the butter and add the flour. Cook slowly, stirring all the time, until the flour has absorbed all the butter – it must not brown.

Stir in boiling milk, a little at a time. Keep stirring until the mixture comes to the boil again and thickens. Add salt, pepper and a good pinch of nutmeg. Simmer on a very low heat for 15 – 20 minutes. Remove from the heat. Add egg, if using, and beat quickly so that the egg does not curdle. Keep warm.

Once the béchamel sauce is ready, assemble the moussaka. Grate plenty of cheese. I usually use strong cheddar. At the bottom of an ovenproof dish, one from which you can serve, put a thin layer of meat sauce, then a layer of fried aubergines, a layer of béchamel sauce, a layer of cheese and so on until the dish is full, finishing with béchamel sauce and a generous layer of cheese. At this point, it can be frozen. Otherwise bake in a medium oven at 180 °C/ 350 °F/Gas 4 for about 45 minutes, until cheese is bubbly and brown. Let stand for 10 minutes before serving.

VARIATION

■ I do not always use this elaborate method above for the béchamel sauce as time does not always permit. The following method tastes equally good:

Boil the milk together with the butter, 5 ml (1 tsp) salt, 2.5 ml (½ tsp) pepper and nutmeg. Mix 12.5 ml (2½ tsp) cornflour with enough milk to bind, making sure it is smooth and lump-free. When the milk boils, stir in the cornflour vigorously, so that no lumps form. Remove from stove and add lightly-beaten egg, mixing all the while so that the egg does not curdle. Return to stove and simmer on low heat for 1 – 2 minutes. I use this method for many recipes that call for a white sauce. You can omit the egg, but it does enhance the flavour of the sauce. Continue with the recipe as above.

If you do not want the moussaka to be too rich you can just add béchamel sauce and grated cheese to the top rather than adding them to the layers.

maqli batenghen

plain fried aubergines

SERVES 6

Prepare aubergines as for *moussaka* (see p. 90), but cut into thick slices. Fry them in hot oil until brown, then drain well. Alternatively, sprinkle them with flour and deep-fry. Aubergines cooked in this way are very good served with fried fish and tartare sauce.

masbaht el darweesh

oven-baked aubergines

Here is another good method of using this delectable vegetable. In this recipe, the round aubergines are as suitable as the elongated ones.

SERVES 4

2 large onions, thinly sliced
25 g (1 oz) butter
450 g (1 lb) boneless lamb, cubed
200 g (7 oz) aubergines, cubed
200 g (7 oz) courgettes, cubed
200 g (7 oz) potatoes, cubed
2 tomatoes, chopped
salt and pepper
250 ml (8 fl oz) water

Fry onions in butter until softened. Add the meat and fry until browned. Add the aubergines, courgettes, potatoes and tomatoes. Season with salt and pepper. Place in a shallow dish with a lid. Add water and bake, covered, at 180 °C/350 °F/Gas 4 until all moisture is absorbed.

sheik al mahshi

baked aubergines with tomato sauce

SERVES 6

8 thin, long aubergines
butter or vegetable oil
2 large onions
1 kg (2¼ lb) lamb, minced
salt and pepper
5 ml (1 tsp) ground mixed spice
50 g (2 oz) pine nuts, fried in a little butter or oil
450 g (1 lb) tomatoes, skinned and chopped
2 tomatoes, sliced

Leave the skin on the aubergines or, if you prefer, peel off strips of the skin to give a striped effect. Leave the stalk to hold them in shape. Fry slowly in butter or oil, turning occasionally, until soft. Arrange the aubergines in a shallow dish. Meanwhile, heat the butter or oil and fry the onions until soft. Add the lamb and cook until coloured. Add salt and pepper, mixed spice and a little water. Cook gently until the meat is tender. Stir in the pine nuts. In another pot, cook the tomatoes until you have a nice sauce (tomato purée may be used instead if you are short of time.) Chicken or meat stock cubes can also be added to enhance the flavour.

Cut the aubergines lengthways and fill with the meat mixture. Pour the tomato sauce over the stuffed aubergines and top each with a slice of tomato. Bake at 180 °C/350 °F/Gas 4 for about 30 minutes. Serve with rice.

batenghen i kousa

aubergines and courgettes

This dish is delicious hot or cold. The vegetables may also be used individually, if you prefer to omit one or the other.

SERVES 6

900 g (2 lb) aubergines and courgettes
30 ml (2 tbsp) vegetable oil
1 clove garlic, crushed
2 – 3 tomatoes, skinned and chopped
    or grated

salt and pepper
30 ml (2 tbsp) chopped parsley
1 green pepper, chopped (optional)
1 onion (optional)

Cut the aubergines and courgettes into bite-size pieces. Wash, salt and drain in a colander for 30 minutes.

Heat oil and add garlic and vegetables. Cook gently to allow vegetables to soften, stirring once or twice. Add tomatoes, a little salt and pepper and parsley. Add a little water if necessary. Cover and cook gently until all the vegetables are tender. You can also add green pepper and onion, in which case, sauté the onion and green pepper before adding them to the pan with the rest of the vegetables.

batenghen bi hoummus

aubergines with chickpeas

SERVES 6

200 g (7 oz) chickpeas, soaked overnight
650 g (1½ lb) aubergines
vegetable oil

500 g (1¼ lb) onions, chopped
450 g (1 lb) tomatoes, skinned and
    thickly sliced
salt and pepper
2 – 3 cloves garlic, crushed (optional)

Drain and rinse the chickpeas, place in a large saucepan, cover with water and bring to the boil. Cover the pan and simmer for 1 hour. Prepare aubergines as for *moussaka* (see p. 90), but cut into cubes instead of slices. Fry in oil in batches until golden brown. Remove the aubergines and fry onions in the same oil. Put aubergines and onions in a casserole dish, add chickpeas and tomatoes. Season with salt and pepper and add garlic if using. Cover and bake in a medium oven at 170 °C/325 °F/Gas 3 for about 1 hour.

stuffed vegetables

NO DINNER PARTY, wedding, christening, funeral wake or any gathering for that matter, is complete without two or more stuffed dishes. They are normally served at least once or twice during the week and almost always on Sundays, each family varying the ingredients with a little bit of this, a little bit of that.

'A little bit' can mean anything from a teaspoon to a tablespoon or even a cup, as no Lebanese cook can give you exact measurements. I have tried to be as accurate as possible. The fillings for the vegetables are mainly the same, but a few variations are given. When cooking stuffed vegetables in a pot, press an inverted plate over the top of the vegetables. This helps keep them in place.

Rice is usually served with these dishes and they are just as good served cold or hot. There is always a dish of yoghurt on the table to eat with stuffed vegetables.

BASIC STUFFING MIXTURE

Lamb is the most common and best ingredient, but minced beef or veal or a mixture may also be used. Although it is not traditionally used I have also added pork in some of the recipes, for variation. However, lamb remains the best.

200 g (7 oz) long-grain rice	2 ml (⅓ tsp) allspice
salt and pepper	2.5 ml (½ tsp) cinnamon
600 g (1¼ lb) minced meat	a little melted butter (clarified, if possible)

Prepare the rice as on pp. 41–42. Mix all ingredients together in a large dish. Knead well with your hands until the mixture is thoroughly blended.

mahshi batenghen

stuffed aubergines

Long, narrow aubergines are good for stuffing. All Lebanese homes have a long-handled gadget called a *munara* for scooping out the insides of aubergines. If you cannot obtain one, use a potato peeler, apple corer or a spoon. Cut the top off the aubergine just below the stalk. Scoop out as much pulp as you can, being careful not to break the skin. Reserve the pulp for salad, stews, mixing in an omelette, adding to stuffing or cooking on its own. Sprinkle the inside of the aubergines with salt, turn upside-down and leave to drain for 30 minutes. Rinse well before stuffing. When adding the filling, be sure to push it right to the bottom. Each aubergine should be only three-quarters full to allow for expansion. Some people fry the aubergines before baking or poaching. This makes a scrumptiously rich dish, but as we are all health-conscious now, it is not necessary. The following three recipes are variations on the basic stuffing for aubergines:

Clockwise from top: Stuffed courgettes (p. 97); Stuffed aubergines (above); Yoghurt (p. 32).

sheik el mahshi batenghen

aubergines with supreme stuffing

SERVES 6

12 long aubergines
salt and freshly ground black pepper
20 g (¾ oz) pine nuts
butter or vegetable oil
basic stuffing mixture (see p. 94)

30 – 45 ml (2 – 3 tbsp) tomato purée
50 ml (2 fl oz) boiling water
50 ml (2 fl oz) vegetable oil (optional)
juice of 1 lemon
1 chicken or beef stock cube (optional)
2 tomatoes, sliced (optional)

Prepare the aubergines as described on p. 94. Brown the pine nuts in butter or oil and add filling. Stuff the aubergines three-quarters full. If desired, put back caps that were cut off. Arrange in a large saucepan.

Mix the tomato purée with the boiling water and pour over the aubergines, adding more water if necessary to cover. If you have not fried the aubergines, add the oil. Add 5 ml (1 tsp) salt and the lemon juice, cover and simmer until cooked – about 45 minutes.

Alternatively, you can bake the stuffed aubergines in an ovenproof dish, in which case, mix the same quantities of tomato purée and boiling water, then crumble in the stock cube. Add sufficient water to come halfway up the aubergines. Add the juice of a lemon, arrange tomato slices on top and drizzle oil all over. Bake in a hot oven at 180 °C/350 °F/Gas 4 for about 45 minutes.

batenghen m'lubis b'lagham

aubergines wrapped in meat

SERVES 6

600 g (1¼ lb) minced meat
2 ml (⅓ tsp) allspice
2.5 ml (½ tsp) cinnamon
5 – 10 ml (1 – 2 tsp) ground cumin
fresh mint, chopped, or dried mint, crumbled

1 hot chilli, chopped (optional)
1 small green pepper, finely chopped
    (optional)
a little melted butter
12 long, thin aubergines
butter for frying

To make the 'wrapping', combine the meat, spices, chilli, green pepper and melted butter. Wash aubergines, but do not scoop them out. Fry them in butter, then drain on paper towels. Flatten the stuffing with a fork. Pat it around each aubergine to 'wrap' it. Arrange in a casserole, add the tomato sauce as in 'aubergines with supreme stuffing' (see above) and simmer for about 45 minutes, or until cooked.

kousa mahshi
stuffed courgettes

For a fabulously rich dish you can fry the courgettes before poaching them.

SERVES 6 – 8

18 – 20 medium-sized courgettes
basic stuffing mixture (see p. 94)
1 onion, sliced (optional)
2 tomatoes, sliced
30 – 45 ml (2 – 3 tbsp) tomato purée
60 ml (2½ fl oz) boiling water
juice of 1 lemon
1 chicken stock cube (optional)
salt and pepper
2 – 3 cloves garlic
dried mint

Wash courgettes and scoop out centre using an apple corer. Start at the stem end and work the corer gently round, turning courgette and the corer at the same time. You must work gently as courgettes pierce easily. Remove as much pulp as possible. If they are bitter, salt them and let them drain for 30 minutes. Half-fill the courgettes with stuffing, do not use too much stuffing as the courgettes will burst when cooking.

Lightly fry the onion and lay at the bottom of a large pot. Cover with a layer of tomato slices and then arrange courgettes on top. Mix the tomato purée with boiling water and pour over courgettes. Squeeze over lemon juice. Here I add a chicken stock cube. I know that traditional Lebanese cooks may frown upon this, but it definitely improves the flavour. Sprinkle on a little salt and pepper. If desired, add a few tomato slices. Leave to simmer very gently for about 1 hour. Just before the courgettes are cooked, crush garlic with a little salt and lemon juice and sprinkle over the courgettes, along with crumbled dried mint.

VARIATION
■ This dish is delicious cooked in yoghurt. Instead of cooking the courgettes in the tomato stew, prepare yoghurt as for soup (see p. 40). Bring to the boil. Prepare and stuff the courgettes as above and add them to the soup. Just before they are cooked, fry some crushed garlic in butter until golden and add to the soup with some dried mint.

Courgettes can also be stuffed with a mixture similar to *tabbouleh* (see p. 112), but use rice instead of cracked wheat. This looks lovely when the courgettes are cut in half lengthways.

mahshi batatis bi sanieh

stuffed potatoes

Stuffed onions, sweet peppers and tomatoes may be cooked with the potatoes. Ensure that you have sufficient filling for all the vegetables.

SERVES 6 –10

10 – 12 medium-sized potatoes
25 g (1 oz) butter or butter and vegetable
    oil mixed
50 g (2 oz) pine nuts (optional)
600 g (1¼ lb) minced lamb or beef topside

1 onion, finely chopped
salt and pepper
2 ml (¼ tsp) allspice
2 ml (¼ tsp) cinnamon
45 ml (3 tbsp) tomato purée
500 ml (17 fl oz) boiling water

Peel potatoes and make a fairly large hole in them with an apple corer or the back of a spoon. Heat the butter or butter and oil and sauté the potatoes for a few minutes. This is not strictly necessary but it does make for a far superior and shamefully delicious taste. Remove from heat and set aside.

Fry the pine nuts, if using, in the same pot, adding more butter if necessary. Remove with a slotted spoon. Add the meat to the pot, squashing with a fork to remove lumps. Add the onions, salt and pepper, spices and pine nuts. Put a sprinkling of water over the mixture to keep it moist and cook for 15 – 20 minutes.

Stuff the potatoes with the meat mixture and stand them in a single layer in an oven dish. Dilute the tomato purée with boiling water. Cover the potatoes with the tomato sauce. Bake for about 1 hour at 180 °C/350 °F/Gas 4 until tender but not too soft.

Stuffed potatoes, tomatoes and peppers (above).

warah einab mahshi

stuffed vine leaves

If you can, use fresh leaves, picked before they become tough. Wash carefully. I usually make this dish when my vine leaves look good enough to eat, picking, washing, rolling and eating them the same day. If you can't get fresh leaves, use those preserved in brine. Vine leaves in brine are sold in packets or tins. Both are usually good and, deceptively, hold more leaves than one realizes. I found this out when visiting my brother and his wife, who is not Lebanese. My sister-in-law had arranged a Lebanese dinner party and specifically wanted to serve vine leaves. I was not keen to use the tinned variety, suspecting they would be inadequate. But as usual she got her own way. Imagine my surprise on opening the tin to find a tightly-packed roll of leaves that seemed never-ending. They made a fair amount and were very good.

MAKES 36 – 40

vine leaves
basic stuffing mixture (see p. 94)

2 – 3 cloves garlic, crushed
dried mint
juice of 1 lemon
30 ml (2 tbsp) vegetable oil

Prepare fresh leaves by plunging them, a few at a time, into boiling water. If using preserved leaves, put them in a large bowl and pour over boiling water, allowing them to stand for about 20 minutes. Rinse thoroughly under cold running water. Drain.

Place a vine leaf on a plate, vein side up. Place about 15 ml (1 tbsp) of stuffing on it, fold the end and the sides towards the centre, roll and squeeze gently in your palm. The rolls should resemble thin cigars. Line the bottom and sides of a pot with any leftover vine leaves to prevent sticking. Add the rolls in layers, sprinkling crushed garlic, dried mint and lemon juice between the layers. Cover with water mixed with the oil. Place a plate on top of the vine leaves to stop them rising to the top. Simmer slowly until cooked – about 2 hours.

The cooked leaves look very good when turned out from the pot onto a plate. Hold a plate over the pot, turn upside down and gently unmould onto the plate. This dish is equally good cold or hot and it is delicious served with yoghurt.

malfouf mahshi

stuffed cabbage leaves

This dish is a firm favourite with my family.

SERVES 30 – 35

1 large cabbage
basic stuffing mixture (see p. 94)
dried mint

8 – 12 whole garlic cloves
salt and pepper
30 – 45 ml (2 – 3 tbsp) tomato purée (optional)
2 – 3 tomatoes, sliced
juice of 2 lemons

Undo the cabbage gently, leaf by leaf, trying not to tear them. Wash. Keep a few outside leaves to line saucepan. Have boiling, salted water ready in a large pot. Cook the leaves in the water, a few at a time for about 5 – 7 minutes, until leaves become soft. As they are cooked, transfer to a colander to drain.

Cut off the hard central vein. If the leaves are too big, cut to size. Place about 15 ml (1 tbsp) of the filling on each leaf, then fold the sides and roll up. Line the bottom of a saucepan with the unused outside leaves. This prevents the rolls from sticking to the pan. Layer the rolls neatly, adding crushed dried mint and lots of whole garlic cloves between the layers. If desired, you can put in a whole head of garlic. Add salt and pepper. Add water or diluted tomato purée, if preferred, and arrange tomato slices on top. Add lots of lemon juice, as this dish should taste quite sharp. Cover and simmer for about 1 hour.

VARIATIONS

■ This is my own take on the classic dish. Fry some thick lamb chops until browned. Sprinkle them with salt and pepper, then put them on top of the outer cabbage leaves lining the bottom of the pot. Arrange the rolls on top, with dried mint, garlic and lightly-fried onion rings between them. Add diluted tomato purée and a chicken stock cube and top with tomato slices. Serve with a salad.

■ The following is a combination of the Lebanese and the Yugoslav version of stuffed cabbage leaves. (My family call it 'Cabbage roll à la Mommy'.)

Prepare the stuffed cabbage leaves as above, with or without the meat, but with the tomato purée, fried onions and mint, and adding sauerkraut (tinned, undrained) between the layers. If you do not want it too sour, drain and wash the sauerkraut. I usually use it straight from the tin as we enjoy the flavour.

baba gha'noush

aubergines with sesame paste

This can also be served as a dip with hors d'oeuvres.

SERVES 6 – 8

1 – 2 large aubergines
2 – 3 cloves garlic
sesame paste (tahini)
40 g (1½ oz) parsley, chopped

juice of 1 – 2 lemons
chopped parsley and paprika to garnish

Wash and dry aubergines thoroughly and prick them all over with a fork. Place on a baking tray and leave overnight in a cool oven at 120 °C/250 °F/Gas ½, or bake in a hot oven at 200 °C/400 °F/Gas 6 until soft and bubbly. Peel aubergines. Mash the flesh or put in a food processor. If using a processor, process with garlic and remaining ingredients, adding sesame paste gradually, and beating all the time. Alternatively, mash with a fork or potato masher, then add crushed garlic and remaining ingredients to form a smooth paste. The mixture should be quite sour. Garnish and serve.

fattoush

bread salad

SERVES 6 – 8

flat Lebanese bread, pitta or 4 thin slices of
    white bread
juice of 1 – 2 lemons
3 – 4 tomatoes, chopped
1 medium onion or 1 bunch spring onions,
    finely chopped
1 lettuce

1 large or 2 small cucumbers
100 g (4 oz) mixed fresh mint and parsley,
    chopped
1 – 2 cloves garlic, crushed (optional)
salt and pepper
2.5 ml (½ tsp) allspice
125 ml (4 fl oz) sunflower or olive oil

Cube bread and brown under grill. Put in a bowl with lemon juice, tomatoes and onions. Add 1 finely-broken-up lettuce, sliced cucumber, chopped mint and parsley, and crushed garlic, if using. Add salt, pepper, allspice and oil. Mix and enjoy.

Bread salad (above) and Spinach pies (p. 30).

Tomato salad (below) and sliced cucumber; *Taratoor* made with avocado (p. 49).

banadura salatit

tomato salad

SERVES 6 – 8

6 tomatoes
½ cucumber (optional)
½ green pepper (optional)

3 spring onions (optional)
salt and pepper
juice of ½ lemon
sunflower or olive oil

Chop tomatoes into fairly small pieces. They can be served on their own or you can add chopped cucumber, green pepper and spring onions. Dress with salt, pepper, a little lemon juice and oil.

VARIATION

■ Slice tomatoes in rounds and layer in a dish. Over each layer sprinkle chopped spring onions or thin rounds of onion. Add a little parsley and fresh or dried mint, lemon juice, salt and pepper and oil. Do not toss or mix. This goes well with curried dishes.

salatah sbaanegh

spinach salad

SERVES 6 – 8

600 g (1¼ lb) spinach
1 onion or 1 bunch of spring onions, chopped
salt and pepper
pinch of allspice

2.5 ml (½ tsp) cinnamon
5 ml (1 tsp) ground cumin
15 ml (1 tbsp) lemon juice
30 ml (2 tbsp) sunflower or olive oil
15 ml (1 tbsp) chopped parsley

If using large-leafed spinach, remove and discard thick stalks. Wash and dry thoroughly. Chop spinach finely, put in a bowl and add chopped onion, salt, pepper, allspice, cinnamon, cumin, lemon juice, oil and chopped parsley.

ful-nabed

white broad bean salad

SERVES 6 – 8

400 g (14 oz) dried broad beans, soaked
    overnight
2 onions, finely chopped
45 ml (3 tbsp) sunflower or olive oil

600 ml (1 pint) water
15 ml (1 tbsp) lemon juice
salt and pepper
crushed garlic (optional)
15 ml (1 tbsp) chopped parsley
paprika or cayenne pepper to garnish

Drain and rinse the beans. In a large saucepan fry onions gently in 30 ml (2 tbsp) of the oil for 5 minutes until they are soft. Add the water and bring to the boil. Add drained beans, bring to the boil, cover and simmer slowly for 1½ hours, until very soft. Add more water if necessary. The water should be almost simmered away by the end of cooking time.

Mash beans (or use a food processor) to a purée. Add lemon juice, remaining oil, salt and pepper and, if using, garlic. Put purée in a serving dish, drizzle with oil, sprinkle with parsley and garnish with paprika or cayenne pepper.

salatah el loobyea

green bean salad

SERVES 4

1 – 2 cloves garlic
15 ml (1 tbsp) lemon juice
salt and pepper
30 ml (2 tbsp) sunflower or olive oil
1 onion, thinly sliced
600 g (1¼ lb) young green beans

Prepare a dressing of crushed garlic, lemon juice, salt, pepper, oil and onion in a serving dish. Let the onion marinate in the dressing for a while. Use young green beans left whole. If too long break into 2 or 3 pieces. Cook until tender then drain. Add the hot beans to the dressing and stir to coat well. Let cool. Serve or refrigerate until required.

adas salatah

lentil salad

The large, flat brown lentils are best. Place the lentils in a large saucepan, cover with water and bring to the boil. Cover the pan and simmer for 50 minutes until tender. Drain well. Dress as for green bean salad (above).

hindbeh m'tabbal

frisée lettuce salad

SERVES 6 – 8

1 large frisée lettuce (curly endive) (spinach leaves may be substituted – use the stalks as well)

1 onion, finely chopped
salt and pepper
juice of 1 lemon
65 ml (4 tbsp) oil (olive oil, preferably)

Wash leaves thoroughly and chop roughly. Put into boiling water and simmer until soft. Meanwhile, put chopped onion, salt, pepper, lemon juice and oil into a salad bowl. Add cooked, drained lettuce whilst still hot and toss. Leave to cool. Refrigerate.

salatah malfouf

cabbage salad

SERVES 6 – 8

1 white or red cabbage

salt and pepper
35 ml (2 tbsp) lemon juice
45 ml (3 tbsp) sunflower or olive oil

Shred cabbage finely, discarding core and any tough veins. Wash thoroughly. Sprinkle with salt and rub in with your hands until the cabbage is well-coated. Place in a colander. Cover with a weighted plate and leave for about 30 minutes to extract all moisture. The cabbage should become soft. Squeeze the cabbage tightly between your hands to remove all moisture. Place in a salad bowl, add lemon juice, oil, pepper and salt, if needed. Toss well.

VARIATION

■ If you want a crisper salad, shred the cabbage as above and put into a colander with lots of ice cubes. Leave for about 30 minutes. Discard all unmelted ice and bruise cabbage with a mallet or pestle – this brings out the flavour. Squeeze cabbage to remove any excess moisture. Add to the salad bowl with a mixture of garlic crushed with salt, and dress with lemon juice, oil, salt and pepper.

salatah avokaeta

avocado salad

This can also be served as a dip with mezze.

SERVES 6 – 8

2 avocados
1 clove garlic
salt and pepper
15 ml (1 tbsp) lemon juice
15 ml (1 tbsp) olive oil
chopped parsley and paprika to garnish

Use good, ripe avocados, peeled and mashed with a fork, potato masher or food processor. Mash the garlic with salt, add lemon juice (the mixture must be quite sharp), pepper and oil. Combine with the avocado and put into a glass serving bowl, making patterns across the surface with a fork. Garnish with parsley and paprika.

tabbouleh

cracked wheat salad

Wheat salad looks particularly colourful served in a glass bowl. Place the bowl on an oval or round platter and surround with crisp, unbroken lettuce leaves. To eat, place a lettuce leaf on a serving plate, drop the salad into the middle of the leaf and fold the lettuce over like a parcel.

SERVES 6 – 8

200 g (7 oz) cracked wheat soaked in water
    for 30 minutes
1 large bunch parsley, well washed and
    thoroughly dried
1 – 2 bunches spring onions or 1 fairly large
    onion
few sprigs of fresh mint
15 – 30 ml (1 – 2 tbsp) dried mint

1 – 2 gherkins, finely chopped (optional)
1 small green pepper (optional)
salt and pepper
pinch of allspice
2.5 ml (½ tsp) cinnamon
5 ml (1 tsp) ground cumin (optional)
juice of 1 – 2 lemons
approx. 60 ml (4 tbsp) oil (olive oil preferably)
3 – 4 tomatoes

Squeeze the wheat well with your hands, making sure all moisture is removed. Put in a bowl. Finely chop parsley (remove thick stalks), onions and mint. This can be done in a food processor. Add to the bowl, together with dried mint, greens, gherkin, green pepper, if using, salt, pepper and spices and refrigerate until needed. Just before serving, finely chop the tomatoes and add with the lemon juice and oil. Mix and taste for seasoning.

salatit batatas

potato salad

SERVES 6 – 8

1 kg (2¼ lb) potatoes
1 – 2 cloves garlic
15 ml (1 tbsp) lemon juice

salt and pepper
30 ml (2 tbsp) sunflower or olive oil
1 onion, thinly sliced
chopped parsley to garnish

Boil 1 kg (2¼ lb) potatoes in their jackets. Prepare dressing as for green bean salad (see p. 110). While potatoes are still hot, slice, then toss in dressing and garnish with parsley. Serve warm or leave to cool.

Cracked wheat salad (above).

salatah khodar

cooked vegetable salad

This recipe can be prepared with any cooked vegetable, e.g. courgettes, cauliflower, beans, etc., mixed together or served on their own.

SERVES 6 – 8

600 g (1¼ lb) cooked vegetables of your
   choice
1 – 2 cloves garlic
salt and pepper
15 ml (1 tbsp) lemon juice
60 ml (4 tbsp) sunflower or olive oil
1 onion, chopped

4 tomatoes, chopped
dried mint or chopped basil to garnish

Cook the vegetables until tender but crispy. Have your salad dressing ready – crush the garlic with salt, pepper, lemon juice and half the oil. Fry the onions and tomatoes in the remaining oil. Add hot, drained vegetables. Toss well. Allow to cool. Sprinkle with crushed dried mint or chopped fresh basil.

satah el loubien yeb-see

butter bean salad

SERVES 6 – 8

250 g (9 oz) dried butter beans, soaked
   overnight

1 – 2 cloves garlic
15 ml (1 tbsp) lemon juice
salt and pepper
30 ml (2 tbsp) sunflower or olive oil
1 onion, thinly sliced

Drain and rinse the beans. Place in a large saucepan, cover with water and bring to the boil. Cover the pan and simmer for 1 hour until tender. Drain well. Prepare dressing as for green bean salad (see p. 110) and serve. Canned butter beans may also be used.

sweets, preserves
& refreshing drinks

IT IS NOT really the custom among the Lebanese to have a pudding at the end of a meal.
Fruit or compote with yoghurt may be served but most people like to finish off the meal
with yoghurt alone. Nevertheless, we do have some tempting desserts. I have never lost my
love for cornflour and my children used to love it as a hot drink, especially in winter, instead
of cocoa. Most puddings are made from cornflour, ground rice or semolina, very often
saturated with a syrup made of sugar and water, some lemon juice and orange blossom or
rose water.

khoshaf

dried fruit salad

Adding compressed apricots to this dessert gives a thicker juice.

SERVES 6 – 8

1 kg (2¼ lb) dried fruit
60 g (2½ oz) unsalted pistachios (optional)
100 g (4 oz) almonds

15 ml (1 tbsp) orange blossom water or
    Cointreau
15 ml (1 tbsp) rose water
sugar (optional)
pomegranate seeds to decorate

Wash fruit and add the rest of the ingredients. If you wish to sweeten the dish, add sugar to taste. Mix well and leave to draw in its own juice for 1 – 2 days. Decorate with pomegranate seeds.

haûh bi loz

prunes with nuts

The first time I tasted this mouthwatering dessert was at a Greek friend's house, but I have since learned that it is a popular sweet in Lebanon as well. Dried apricots prepared in this way are just as good.

SERVES 3 – 4

16 prunes, pitted
hot tea, freshly made

walnuts, almonds or pecan nuts
sugar
lemon juice or red wine
cream, whipped

Wash the prunes, cover with boiling tea and leave overnight. Strain. Stuff each prune with half a walnut, almond or pecan nut. Traditionally they are simmered in sugared water with lemon juice, but when I had them they were stewed in red wine and sugar. Allow to cool, smother in whipped cream and chill.

Dried fruit salad (above).

balouza

cornflour

Traditionally, cornflour is made with water, but I prefer it with milk. Here is the traditional method – replace the water with milk if you prefer.

SERVES 4 – 6

1.25 litres (2¼ pints) water
sugar to taste

60 g (2½ oz) cornflour
45 ml (3 tbsp) orange blossom or rose water
nuts and pomegranate seeds (optional) to decorate

Bring 1 litre (1¾ pints) water and sugar to the boil. Meanwhile, mix the cornflour to a smooth paste with the remaining water. Add this to the boiling sugar water, stirring all the time. As the mixture boils, beat more vigorously. Reduce heat and simmer, stirring constantly, for about 5 minutes until it has a creamy consistency. Remove from the stove and add the orange blossom water. Pour into individual serving bowls. Cool and chill.

Sprinkle with plenty of nuts, pistachios are the traditional choice. You can even add whole nuts to the mixture. A sprinkling of pomegranate seeds looks most delightful as the red contrasts beautifully with the white. Alternatively, sprinkle the cornflour with cinnamon.

balouza m'hal'la beeyeh

cornflour with milk (as a drink)

Follow the recipe above, but omit the nuts and use 10 ml (2 tsp) cornflour per 250 ml (8 fl oz) milk. Add 5 ml (½ tsp) sugar and serve hot in mugs on a cold day.

Prunes with cream (p. 119) and Cornflour (above).

basbousa

semolina pudding

Semolina makes an absolutely divine dessert and was at one time quite abundant – our home was never without it.

SERVES 4

syrup
600 ml (1 pint) water
15 ml (1 tbsp) lemon juice
600 g (1¼ lb) sugar
5 ml (1 tsp) rose or orange blossom water

pudding
225 g (8 oz) unsalted butter
125 g (4½ oz) semolina
5 ml (1 tsp) cinnamon

To make the syrup, boil water, lemon juice and sugar for about 10 minutes and then add rose or orange blossom water. Meanwhile, make the pudding. Melt the butter until all froth has disappeared. Add semolina slowly and fry for about 5 minutes, stirring all the time. Add syrup and stir well. Cook for a further 2 – 3 minutes. Leave to stand for about 10 minutes. Serve sprinkled with cinnamon and with lots of thick cream or *eishta* (see p. 122). For variation, add yoghurt or toasted nuts.

mowz wa laban

banana and yoghurt pudding

Stoned dates can also be added to this dessert and the yoghurt replaced with lightly whipped cream.

SERVES 4 – 6

600 – 900 ml (1 – 1½ pints) yoghurt

3 – 4 bananas
sugar to taste

Beat yoghurt until creamy. Slice the bananas into it and gently mix until they are well coated. Add sugar if desired.

Banana and yoghurt pudding with dates and Semolina pudding (above).

sweetmeats

IT IS SAID that in a year in which there are plenty of almonds and dates, there will also be increased prosperity in life.

The Lebanese have a very sweet tooth and gourmets agree with me that some of the finest sweetmeats and pastries come from the Middle East. I must confess that it is only recently that I have attempted these mysterious goodies and have been pleasantly surprised to discover how easy they are to make. I have always been spoilt because my aunt, who usually made the 'lovers' shortbread' when the need arose, is famous for this melt-in-the-mouth confection. But then she is famous for all her cooking, as were her sisters, who have regrettably passed away. From her I learned the art of Lebanese cooking and she, of course, was taught by my much-loved grandmother. My childhood friend, Mona, who is a master in the art of baking has also always spoilt me with semolina cookies and other mouthwatering cakes, and has taught her daughters so well that she herself hardly needs to bake at all these days.

Many of the sweetmeats and cakes are saturated in a syrup, so I will begin with this recipe.

atr

syrup

This syrup is traditionally perfumed with orange blossom or rose water which are obtainable from large supermarket or specialist shops. If you cannot find them, do not let this prevent you from making the sweetmeats, as lemon juice will suffice. The uninitiated will not realize that there is something missing. Use whenever a recipe calls for syrup. The usual proportions are as follows, unless otherwise stated.

MAKES 600–750 ML (1–1¼ PINT) SYRUP

450 g (1 lb) sugar

300 ml (½ pint) water
15 ml (1 tbsp) lemon juice
15 ml (1 tbsp) orange blossom or rose water

Bring sugar, water and lemon juice to the boil and cook vigorously for 5 minutes until thick. The mixture should coat the back of a spoon. Add the orange blossom or rose water. Allow to cool and chill.

a'tayif

pancakes

Pancakes are popular the world over and we all have our favourite recipe for making them. If you ask a Lebanese cook for their recipe, the answer will be 'a little bit of this, a little bit of that'. I have yet to get a Lebanese recipe from someone with exact measurements. Invariably, it is a small teacup or so many teacups of whatever. Lebanese cooks measure from experience, adding their favourite extras. Try this version as it is very good. Serve with the usual syrup (see p. 128).

MAKES 30

15 ml (1 tbsp) fresh yeast or 7 ml (1½ tsp) easy-blend dried yeast
500 ml (17 fl oz) warm water
5 ml (1 tsp) sugar

350 g (12 oz) plain flour, sifted
5 ml (1 tsp) oil
5 ml (1 tsp) salt
chilled syrup (see p. 128)
cream
chopped nuts (preferably pistachios)

Dissolve yeast in 125 ml (4 fl oz) of the warm water, and add sugar and 1 teaspoon flour. Mix and let stand in a warm place for about 10 minutes until frothy. Put sifted flour into mixing bowl and make a hole in the centre. Pour yeast into the flour, add the oil and salt and work in, gradually adding the balance of the water, stirring continuously until the mixture is nice and smooth. Cover and let stand in a warm place for 1 hour. The mixture will bubble and rise.

Heat a greased frying pan until very hot. If you are using a non-stick pan, oil is unnecessary. Reduce heat to low. Pour about 30 ml (2 tbsp) batter into the pan, tilting to let it spread evenly but not too thinly. When bubbly, loosen with a spatula and turn gently. Dip into cold syrup and serve with cream, sprinkled with chopped nuts.

a-tayif bi gebna

pancakes with cheese

Prepare batter as above. Fry one side only. Put a layer of unsalted cheese on the uncooked side, fold in half in traditional half-moon shapes, press edges together and fry in hot oil until crisp and golden. Remove with a slotted spoon and drop into cold syrup (see p. 128). Serve hot.

You can prepare the batter in advance. Fry just before serving.

a-tayif bi loz

pancakes with nuts

For extra calories and enjoyment, serve these pancakes with whipped cream. They can also be filled with *eishta* (see p. 122).

MAKES 30

pancake batter (see p. 129)
oil for frying

225 g (8 oz) pistachios, walnuts or other nuts
30 ml (2 tbsp) sugar
10 ml (2 tsp) cinnamon
cold syrup (see p. 128)

Heat a greased frying pan and pour about 30 ml (2 tbsp) batter into the pan. Fry one side only. Sprinkle the unfried side with nuts, sugar and cinnamon. Fold into half-moon shapes, press together and fry in hot oil. Drain and, while still hot, drop into cold syrup.

ghreest el loz

semolina cookies

As this sweetmeat does not keep well in tins, leave in pan, cover and remove as needed. Semolina cookies freeze well. Open-freeze and, when frozen, pack in polythene bags. You can also put half the mixture in the pan, spread with coarsely-chopped nuts, then pat the rest of the mixture evenly over the top and smooth as before. Or you can use unsalted cheese in the middle, but this must be eaten the same day as the cheese hardens if left standing. It is a delicious dessert. The taste of the cheese and syrup blend well together.

MAKES 75 – 80

900 g (2 lb) semolina
10 ml (2 tsp) baking powder
120 g (4½ oz) plain flour

350 g (12 oz) butter
about 250 ml (8 fl oz) milk
almonds
chilled syrup (see p. 128)

Mix dry ingredients together. Melt butter, add to dry ingredients and combine well. Add milk and mix to a thick pouring consistency. If needed, add more milk. Put into baking tray about 20 x 30 cm (8 x 12 in) in size and smooth mixture down well. Dip hand into milk and smooth over top. Cut into traditional diamond shapes, slicing about 4 cm (1½ in) deep. Put half an almond in the centre of each diamond. Bake in a preheated oven at 190 °C/375 °F/Gas 5 for 45 minutes – 1 hour. Cut shapes right through. Pour the cold syrup over the sweetmeats while they are still hot.

Clockwise from top left: Semolina cookies (above); Variety of filo pastry sweetmeats (pp. 141–143); 'Shredded wheat' sweetmeats; Lovers' shortbread (p. 132).

ghuraybee

Lovers' shortbread

These melt-in-the-mouth, buttery shortbreads are much easier to make than one would imagine. The die-hards insist on beating by hand, but the result is just as good when beaten in an electric mixer. I must tell you that using clarified butter makes a tremendous difference, but most people today use ordinary butter. Anyway, go ahead and try them. Be sure to be prepared for cries of 'more please', but they do keep indefinitely in an airtight container. Crushed pistachios or walnuts can be added to the dough mixture.

MAKES 50

450 g (1 lb) very soft, unsalted butter (clarified if possible)
130 g (4¾ oz) icing sugar, sifted

125 g (4½ oz) cornflour, sifted
500 g (1⅛ lb) plain flour, sifted
almonds
icing sugar for sprinkling

Cream butter until it becomes white and then add icing sugar (you can add half caster to half icing sugar). Beat until light and creamy. Slowly add cornflour and flour. The cornflour makes the mixture lighter, but all plain flour can be substituted if desired. No liquid is added as it is a very soft dough. If the dough does not hold its shape, add a little more flour.

There are a couple of traditional shapes for this shortbread. The round one is easy while the others take a bit of practice. Break off little balls about walnut-size, flatten in your hands and make a round shape. In the centre of each, put half an almond. For the more popular sausage shape, break off small pieces, roll into a ball, then press into a torpedo shape, broad in the middle and tapering at each end. Put half an almond on top. The two ends of the sausage shape can also be brought together like a doughnut. Whichever shape you choose, the taste is the same. Do not crowd baking trays, as the shortbread spreads slightly. Bake in a preheated oven at 180 °C / 350 °F/Gas 4 for 15 – 20 minutes. The shortbread must not brown, but remain white, soft and melting. If they do brown slightly, they will have a different taste. Cool in a tray.

Pack in airtight containers with greaseproof paper between layers. Serve sprinkled with plenty of icing sugar.

aweimat bi atr (ata 'eet)

fritters in syrup

MAKES 25 – 30

15 ml (1 tbsp) fresh yeast or 7 ml (1½ tsp)
    easy-blend dried yeast
5 ml (1 tsp) sugar
250 ml (8 fl oz) warm water

450 g (1 lb) plain flour
250 ml (8 fl oz) milk
syrup (see p. 128)
oil for deep-frying
icing sugar and cinnamon for sprinkling

Dissolve yeast with sugar, add a little water and leave to ferment. Sift the flour into a large bowl (which is at room temperature warmed slightly). Add remaining water to the yeast and beat well. Gradually add this mixture to the flour, alternating with the milk, beating all the time. The dough should be as soft and thick as a pancake mixture. Cover and let stand until it rises again. Beat once more and, if possible, repeat the procedure, as success lies in resting and beating the mixture several times. Ideally, after the last beating allow it to rest for 1 hour. The syrup must be ice cold.

Heat a little oil about 5 cm (2 in) deep. Beat dough. Have a container of water handy. Take a wet teaspoonful of dough and drop it into the hot oil. Rinse spoon in water and repeat. Do not overcrowd the pan. When fritters rise to the surface, turn them over and fry until golden, then remove with slotted spoon. Drain and drop into ice-cold syrup. They are delicious hot, sprinkled with icing sugar or cinnamon, but also taste good when cold.

yansoun baskaweet

aniseed biscuits

MAKES 15 – 20

500 ml (8½ oz) plain flour
30 ml (2 tbsp) olive oil

water
60 ml (4 tbsp) aniseed or powdered aniseed
100 g (4 oz) sugar
90 g (3½ oz) sesame seeds

Sift flour into mixing bowl. Add oil and mix evenly. Add water, a little at a time, to form a firm dough. Knead the aniseed and sugar into the dough. Break off little balls, about walnut size. Roll in the sesame seeds, covering well. Place on a greased baking sheet and bake in a preheated oven at 180 °C/350 °F/Gas 4 for about 30 minutes. Cool and pack in an airtight container, as these keep for weeks.

asebeh el arous

bride's fingers

MAKES 15 – 20

240 g (8½ oz) self-raising flour
water
1 egg, lightly beaten

30 g (2 tbsp) walnuts
5 – 10 ml (1 – 2 tsp) cinnamon
100 g (4 oz) sugar
oil for deep-frying
icing sugar for sprinkling

Sift flour and mix with a little water until a firm dough is formed. Work the dough with the lightly-beaten egg. Roll out thinly on a floured board. Cut into strips about 5 x 7.5 cm (2 x 3 in). Pound the nuts and mix with the cinnamon and sugar. Put 5 ml (1 tsp) of the nut mixture along one end of each strip. Fold the sides towards the middle, then roll to form a cigar shape. Pinch edges to seal and deep-fry in oil until golden. Drain, cool and sprinkle with icing sugar.

assbeh el sit

Lady Zeinab's fingers

MAKES 15 – 20

125 g (4¼ oz) self-raising flour
pinch of salt
1 egg, lightly beaten
15 ml (1 tbsp) oil

75 ml (3 fl oz) warm water
225 g (8 oz) nuts, preferably walnuts
30 ml (2 tbsp) sugar
melted butter for brushing
chilled syrup (see p. 128)

Sift flour and salt into a mixing bowl. Make a hole in the centre and add the egg and the oil. Mix with a fork and gradually add the warm water. The dough mixture should be soft. Remove to a well-floured pastry board and knead for about 5 minutes. Dip hands in a little oil and rub all around dough. Cover and let stand. Meanwhile, finely chop the nuts. Add sugar. Break off small pieces of dough and roll each piece paper-thin into oblong shapes about 7.5 x 15 cm (3 x 6 in). Trim uneven edges. Place 5 ml (1 tsp) nuts at one end of each shape and roll up lightly into 'fingers'. Place on a well-buttered baking sheet. Brush tops with melted butter. Bake in a preheated oven at 190 °C/375 °F/Gas 5 for about 10 – 15 minutes until light brown. Pour cold syrup over immediately.

sanbusik bi loz

almond patties

I have given two ways of making the dough, see which one works best for you.

MAKES 45 – 50

dough no. 1

600 g (1¼ lb) plain flour

pinch of salt

5 ml (1 tsp) baking powder

115 g (4¼ oz) butter (clarified, if possible)

100 g (4 oz) sugar

125 – 250 ml (4 – 8 fl oz) warm milk or
    water (or a mixture)

nut filling (see below)

icing sugar for sprinkling (optional)

Sift flour, salt and baking powder into a mixing bowl. Rub in butter with fingers, add sugar and milk or water and mix into a soft dough. Roll out fairly thinly and cut into rounds about 7.5 cm (3 in) in diameter. Put filling in the middle and fold into half-moon shapes. Pinch edges together and bake on a flat baking tray in a preheated oven at 240 °C/475 °F/Gas 9 for about 8 minutes, until golden. Serve plain or sprinkle with icing sugar.

dough no. 2

125 ml (4 fl oz) oil

100 g (4 oz) butter (clarified, if possible)

125 ml (4 fl oz) warm water

5 ml (1 tsp) salt

500 g (1½ lb) plain flour, sifted

nut filling (see below)

Put oil and butter in the top of a double boiler. Heat over boiling water until melted. Mix in warm water and salt. Pour into a large mixing bowl.

Gradually add sifted flour, stirring slowly with hands. Use your own judgement as to whether a tablespoon or more of flour is necessary. Dough mixture must be a soft, greasy ball. Do not handle the dough too much, so stop mixing as soon as it holds together. Take walnut-size pieces and flatten out as thinly as possible between the palms of your hands or, alternatively, roll out as thin as possible and cut into about 7.5-cm (3-in) rounds with a pastry cutter. Put filling in the centre and fold into traditional half-moon shapes. Bake as above.

nut filling

200 g (7 oz) ground almonds or walnuts

225 g (8 oz) icing sugar

30 ml (2 tbsp) orange blossom water

Mix together all the ingredients and use as a filling for almond patties (see above). Alternatively, form into small balls, deep-fry and serve as a sweetmeat.

ka 'e semsem

sesame cookies

MAKES 36 – 40

450 g (1 lb) plain flour
300 g (11 oz) sugar
15 ml (3 tsp) baking powder
pinch of salt

225 g (8 oz) soft butter
2 large eggs, beaten well with 7.5 ml (1½ tsp)
   vanilla essence
125 ml (4 fl oz) oil
sesame seeds

Sift dry ingredients together. Rub in butter until mixture resembles breadcrumbs. Beat in the egg mixture. Knead well, add oil and knead again until dough is soft and pliable. Break off pieces, shape into rounds and roll in sesame seeds, pressing seeds into biscuits. Put on baking trays in a preheated oven at 130 °C/250 °F/Gas 1/2 for 30 – 40 minutes, until lightly browned.

ka 'ek bi balah

date cookies

MAKES 35

450 g (1 lb) plain flour
pinch of salt
water

250 g (9 oz) dates
450 g (1 lb) nuts, chopped
30 g (2 tbsp) grated nutmeg
icing sugar for sprinkling

Mix flour with salt and enough water to form a good firm dough. Roll out thinly on a floured board. Pound dates to a pulp and add nuts. Add nutmeg and mix thoroughly.

   Cut the dough into strips 6 x 8 cm (2½ x 3¼ in) strips. Roll a teaspoon of the date mixture into a finger shape. Place finger in the centre of each strip of dough. Fold over dough and seal edges. Form a ring by bringing the ends together and pinching them firmly. Place on a greased baking tray and bake in a preheated oven at 180 °C /350 °F/Gas 4 for about 40 minutes, until golden. Cool and then sprinkle with icing sugar. These cookies keep well in an airtight container.

Clockwise from top left: *Bahleawah*, filo pasty with nut filling and Lady Zeinab's fingers; Fritters in syrup (p. 133); Mint tea (p. 155); Date cookies (above).

knafie burmah

'shredded wheat' cookies

The special pastry used for these cookies, called *knafie*, can be bought ready-made from Lebanese or Greek delicatessens. The long, thin strands look like fine spaghetti and, when cooked, like shredded wheat.

MAKES 30 – 36

900 g (2 lb) *knafie* 'shredded wheat' pastry
250 g (9 oz) melted butter
600 g (1¼ lb) nuts (pistachios, walnuts, almonds or a mixture)

100 g (4 oz) sugar
30 ml (2 tbsp) orange blossom or rose water
250 ml (8 fl oz) milk

Put the pastry strands into a bowl and separate them with your fingers. Then pour over 250 g (9 oz) melted butter and mix thoroughly, coating each strand. Place half the pastry in an ovenproof dish. Chop nuts and mix with sugar. Spread evenly over pastry. Place the remaining pastry over the top. Mix orange blossom or rose water with milk. Sprinkle over the top, pour on a little melted butter and bake in a preheated oven at 180 °C/350 °F/Gas 4 for about 20 minutes, until all the moisture has evaporated and the pastry is semi-crisp and golden. Serve hot.

VARIATION

■ Omit the orange blossom or rose water and the milk. Bake at 180 °C/350 °F/Gas 4 for about 45 minutes then increase the temperature to 230 °C/450°F/Gas 8 for 10 – 15 minutes. Pour over chilled syrup (see p. 128) and serve hot or cold.

cream filling
500 ml (17 fl oz) milk
20 ml (4 tsp) cornflour

25 g (1 oz) sugar
150 ml (5 fl oz) double cream

Boil half the milk. Mix cornflour, sugar and the remaining milk together until smooth. Add to boiling milk, beating vigorously. Turn heat down and let the mixture simmer, stirring all the time, until very thick. Allow to cool. Remove any skin that has formed. Add cream. Mix well. Use to fill the pastry. This mixture is sufficient for half the amount of dough given above, so double up or cut down the pastry mix.

The pastry can also be filled with cheese. Ricotta is good, but any cheese will do. Bake as before and pour the chilled syrup over the hot pastry. It is a good combination. You can also fill with dates. Prepare date filling as described on p. 136.

VARIATIONS

■ Another method is to make individual rolls filled with nuts. Mix some chopped nuts (pistachios, almonds and walnuts) with sugar and orange blossom or rose water. Take some strands of pastry and form into a bundle. Hollow out the bundle and fill with nut mixture, then close the opening. Arrange on a baking tray and bake at 190 ºC/375 ºF/Gas 5 until golden. Remove from oven and pour over the chilled syrup.

■ For another alternative, take a flat skewer, spread the nut mixture on top and twist the buttered dough threads closely around the sticks as though you are rolling candy floss. Pull the stick out carefully, leaving the filing behind. Bake as before, then pour over the chilled syrup. Cut into individual servings and serve.

labneh hilweh

yoghurt cheesecake

SERVES 6 – 8

125 ml (4 fl oz) yoghurt
65 g (2½ oz) icing sugar

30 g (2 tbsp) powdered gelatine
125 ml (4 fl oz) water
2 packets plain, sweet biscuits

Begin by making your own yoghurt (see p. 32) or use commercial natural yoghurt. Put into a muslin bag and let the whey drain completely. You will then have cream cheese. Put in a bowl and mix in the icing sugar. Dissolve gelatine in the water according to packet instructions. Stir into cheese. In a shallow dish, put a layer of biscuits then add the cheese mixture, so that it is at least 5 cm (2 in) thick. Top with a layer of biscuits. Chill for 1 hour or more until biscuits are soft. Slice and serve.

ka 'ek maqli

fried bread cake

SERVES 6 – 8

2 loaves French bread
2 eggs, beaten

10 ml (2 tsp) vanilla essence
250 ml (8 fl oz) milk
oil for frying
icing sugar for sprinkling

Cut the bread into slices. Mix the eggs, vanilla and milk together in a bowl and dip each slice of bread into the mixture. Fry in deep, hot oil until golden and then drain. Sprinkle with icing sugar and serve.

ama 'amoul

stuffed semolina pastries

This is an Easter speciality. The pastries can be filled with different kinds of nuts or with dates.

MAKES 75 – 80

250 g (9 oz) plain flour
900 g (2 lb) semolina
100 g (4 oz) caster sugar
225 g (8 oz) butter, melted

30 ml (2 tbsp) orange blossom or rose water
250 ml (8 fl oz) milk
250 ml (8 fl oz) water or more milk
nut or date filling (see below)
icing sugar for sprinkling

Sift flour into mixing bowl and add semolina and caster sugar. Use your hands to thoroughly work butter into the mixture. Add orange blossom or rose water, milk and water (you can use all milk and no water, if preferred). Work dough until it is pliable and soft. This can be set aside for a few hours or overnight, but it is not essential.

Break off little bits and shape into balls. Hollow out with your index finger. Add filling and close the top. Arrange on a large baking tray and use a fork to score the top of each pastry. Bake in a preheated oven at 180 °C/350 °F/Gas 4 for about 20 – 30 minutes. Do not brown too much, if at all. While still hot, sprinkle generously with icing sugar. These delectable pastries keep well in an airtight container.

nut filling

200 g (7 oz) walnuts or almonds, finely
    chopped

15 ml (1 tbsp) orange blossom or rose water

Mix together and use to fill the semolina pastries.

date filling

450 g (1 lb) stoneless dates

125 ml (4 fl oz) water
15 ml (1 tbsp) orange blossom water

Chop dates. Place the dates, water and orange blossom water in a saucepan. Cook over a low heat until very soft. Use to fill semolina pastries.

bahlearwah

filo pastry

They say you are not a fully-fledged Lebanese cook until you have made filo pastry. It can be used with so many mouthwatering fillings and is relatively easy to make. The art is to be able to roll it into paper-thin sheets. I have given a small quantity to start with. If you succeed, double up next time. If you don't, store-bought sheets are relatively cheap and are of good quality.

MAKES 24 SHEETS

1.5 kg (3½ lb) plain flour
7.5 ml (1½ tsp) salt
500 ml (17 fl oz) warm water

45 ml (3 tbsp) vegetable oil
cornflour
30 ml (2 tbsp) melted butter
nut filling (see p. 142)
chilled syrup (see p. 128)

Sift flour and salt into a large mixing bowl. Add enough warm water, very slowly, to make a pliable dough. Knead well before pressing down. Push dough forward with the palm of your hand and use your knuckles to fold the dough back on itself. Repeat for about 10 minutes or until the dough can be gathered into a soft ball. Add the oil, a tablespoon at a time. Knead well after each addition and continue until dough is smooth and satiny – about 20 – 25 minutes. Cover bowl with a blanket or a sheet of plastic. Leave in a warm, draught-free place for at least 2 hours. The dough can be left in the fridge for about a week, but must be brought to room temperature before rolling.

To use dough, divide into 20 equal balls. These will be about 40 cm (1½ in) in diameter. Sprinkle a clean cloth with cornflour. On the cloth, roll each ball with a rolling pin into rounds of about 18 cm (7 in) in diameter. As they are rolled, stack between sheets of greaseproof paper. When all pieces have been rolled and stacked, cover with a cloth and let stand for about 30 minutes.

Now the art comes into it. You have to stretch the dough over the back of your hands, lifting it and stretching by pulling your hands apart repeatedly. This has to be done gently and quickly. Some stretch the dough over a cushion covered with a clean cloth. If you are like me, you will have a few thick edges. Just cut them off. Have the melted butter ready to grease a pan of about 30 – 45 cm (12 – 18 in).

As the dough is stretched into paper-thin sheets, butter with a pastry brush and lay in pan. When you have done half, put your filling in and continue buttering the other half. If you would like to make thinner layers, then use two trays, using about six layers around the filling. Trim the sides of any overlapping dough. If you double the sheets in the pan, then butter each fold and count as two. Bake in a preheated oven at 180 °C/350 °F/Gas 4 until light golden and puffed. The layers must be separated and crisp. Alternatively, you can bake in a slow oven at 150 °C /300 °F/ Gas 2 for 90 minutes. Remove and pour over the chilled syrup as soon as it comes out of the oven. Cool in pan.

Unbuttered sheets of filo pastry can be stored indefinitely in the freezer. They must be defrosted slowly and completely before using, otherwise they will crumble. Unwrap one sheet at a time. Butter and layer.

loz

nut filling

Loz strictly means almond, but I usually use pecans and they are delicious.

FILLS 24 PASTRIES

200 g (7 oz) walnuts, pistachios, almonds
    or pecans, coarsely chopped or any mixed
    nuts, except peanuts

30 ml (2 tbsp) sugar (optional)
24 sheets filo pastry (see p. 141)
chilled syrup (see p.128)

Combine nuts and sugar, if using. Spread evenly on top of the pastry sheets. Cover with the other buttered sheets and cut into traditional diamond shapes. I find it easier to cut from corner to corner. Bake at 180 °C/350 °F/Gas 4 and pour over the chilled syrup as soon as you remove the tray from the oven. Leave to cool in the pan. When ready to serve, cut through again and place each piece on a plate.

These sweetmeats go soggy if stored in a tin, but keep fairly well stored in a cake box. These freeze well if not baked, so prepare up to baking stage. It is not necessary to thaw, but bake them a little longer. Pour over the syrup, as before.

boughasha

cigar pastries with nuts

MAKES 18

100 g (4 oz) nuts, finely chopped
40 g (1½ oz) sugar

14 sheets filo pastry (see p. 141)
melted butter (clarified, if possible)
chilled syrup (see p. 128)

Mix nuts and sugar together and set aside. Brush each sheet of filo pastry with melted butter as you go along. Fold each sheet in half, making a double-layered rectangle. Brush the top with butter. Fold over once again and brush the top with butter. Sprinkle about 15 ml (1 tbsp) nuts on top. Roll into a tight cylinder. Transfer to a well-greased baking sheet. Repeat with the remaining sheets.

Bake in the top part of the oven at 200 °C/400 °F/Gas 6 for about 20 minutes, until crisp and a light golden colour. Slide off baking sheet. Cut into 5-cm (2-in) lengths and pour over cold syrup, or brush the tops with syrup. Serve while still hot, passing around the remaining syrup in a jug.

farareer

birds' nest pastries

MAKES 14

100 g (4 oz) nuts (pistachios are traditional)
15 ml (1 tbsp) sugar

14 sheets filo pastry (see p. 141)
30 ml (2 tbsp) melted butter
chilled syrup (see p. 128)

Chop nuts and mix half with the sugar, leaving the other half without. Brush each pastry sheet with butter and fold in half to make a double rectangle. Brush top with butter. Fold over one of the long edges to make an overlap of about 2.5 cm (1 in). Brush the top with butter. Along the length of the fold, spread out a teaspoon of sugar and nut filling. Now shape the birds' nests. Starting at the fold, roll the pastry to within 5 cm (2 in) of the opposite edge. Fold over the short ends. With the filled side facing upwards, lift the ends of the pastry with both hands and join them to make a ring about 7.5 cm (3 in) in diameter. Crumble the loose pastry into the hollow centre of the ring to form a nest.

Arrange the nests on the buttered baking tray. Brush the tops lightly with butter and bake in the top of a preheated oven at 200 °C/400 °F/Gas 6 for about 20 minutes, until crisp and delicately brown. Gently transfer to a large dish and fill the hollows with the remaining nuts. Pour over the chilled syrup or serve syrup separately.

busa

ice-cream dessert

Take a blob of ice-cream, sprinkle on crushed pistachio nuts or walnuts or both, and add a generous sprinkling of your favourite liqueur. This can also be served on a base of meringue. A somewhat extravagant dessert, but generally speaking, the Lebanese do not economise on food, so enjoy it! Are you now convinced about the sweet tooth of the Lebanese?

apple strudel

I have made apple strudel from the mountain bread (see p. 23) and it is excellent. I discovered this when a visitor from Yugoslavia saw the bread and remarked how suitable it would be for paper-thin strudel. We tried it and it worked. Even experts would not know that the pastry was not genuine. This recipe makes two strudels.

SERVES 4 – 6

1 quantity mountain bread dough
125 g (4½ oz) butter, melted
125 g (4½ oz) dried breadcrumbs or cake
    crumbs
50 g (2 oz) caster sugar
6 – 8 Granny Smith apples, peeled, cored and
    cut into rings
30 ml (2 tbsp) lemon juice
50 g (2 oz) sultanas or raisins
50 g (2 oz) chopped walnuts or pecans

Roll dough into 1 thin round. Butter dough using a pastry brush. Sprinkle one end with a layer of crumbs. Sprinkle with caster sugar. Add a generous layer of apples. Pour lemon juice over apples. Sprinkle with more caster sugar. Add sultanas or raisins and nuts. Smear any raw edges with melted butter. Roll up from end with filling. Place on a baking sheet, either straight or bent into a crescent shape. Bake at 190 °C/375 °F/Gas 5 for about 30 – 45 minutes until nicely browned on top. Serve warm with cream. These also freeze well, in which case prepare, but do not bake. There is no need to thaw before baking, but do allow more cooking time.

petits fours

THE FOLLOWING LITTLE sweetmeats have been adopted around the world, under the name of petits fours. I wonder how many people realize that they originated in the Middle East. They are easy to prepare and large quantities can be made. The selection I have chosen includes the ever popular Turkish delight which, despite its name, is a traditional sweet throughout the Middle East.

ka 'ek bi loz

almond sweetmeats

MAKES 12

450 g (1 lb) ground almonds
1 egg white, stiffly beaten

450 g (1 lb) icing sugar
75 – 90 ml (3 – 3½ oz) orange blossom water
halved almonds or chopped nuts (optional)

Mix the ground almonds into the beaten egg white then add the icing sugar. Use enough orange blossom water to bind, roll into little round balls then flatten and shape into traditional diamond shapes. Place an almond half on each or sprinkle with nuts. Bake in a preheated oven at about 150 °C/300 °F/Gas 2 for about 10 minutes. Do not let them brown. They will look soft, but will become firm when cool. They look attractive in little paper cases.

Alternatively, shape them into bracelets by rolling in a thin cigarette shape and bringing the ends together. They will look like baby's bracelets. Sprinkle with nuts and bake as before.

loz eb sukker

sugar-coated almonds

MAKES 20

450 g (1 lb) almonds

225 g (8 oz) sugar
250 ml (8 fl oz) water
60 ml (4 tbsp) orange blossom or rose water

Place almonds in a pan without adding any fat or oil and, being careful not to burn, cook until they are a nice golden colour on both sides. Spread, evenly spaced, on a baking tray. Mix sugar and water, add orange blossom or rose water. Pour over the almonds. Place in a preheated oven at 180 °C /350 °F/Gas 4 for 10 – 15 minutes, until all the liquid has been absorbed and the sugar clings to the almonds. Cool in the tray. Store in an airtight tin.

halawah

semolina sweets

MAKES 60

150 ml (5 fl oz) olive oil

450 g (1 lb) semolina

450 g (1 lb) cornflour

700 ml (1¼ pints) milk

150 ml (5 fl oz) water

450 g (1 lb) sugar

nuts (almonds, pecans or walnuts, optional)

Heat the oil in a heavy-bottomed pan, until a light haze forms. Pour the semolina in a slow, thin stream into the oil, stirring all the time. Mix the cornflour with a little extra cold water to form a smooth paste and add to the pan. Lower the temperature and cook gently for about 20 minutes, stirring occasionally, until all the oil has been absorbed and the semolina turns a light gold. Mix together with the milk and water. Slowly add the sugar to the semolina. Cook gently for about 10 minutes longer, stirring all the time, until mixture holds its shape almost solidly in the spoon. Be careful not to burn. If necessary, put a heat diffuser under the saucepan.

Pour the mixture onto an ungreased baking sheet. Spread and smooth with the back of a wooden spoon. Cool. When firm, cut into squares.

Chopped or whole nuts may be added. Fry them for a few minutes in butter before adding to semolina mixture.

VARIATION

■ If you want a richer taste, make it with sugar water syrup as follows:

600 ml (1 pint) water

600 g (1¼ lb) sugar

5 ml (1 tsp) cinnamon

15 ml (1 tbsp) lemon juice

125 g (4½ oz) semolina

100 g (4 oz) unsalted butter

nuts (optional)

Boil water, sugar, cinnamon and lemon juice for about 10 minutes. Fry the semolina in the butter over a low heat for 5 minutes, stirring all the time. Add the syrup, still stirring, and cook gently for a further 5 minutes. Leave to cool and then cut into squares or traditional diamond shapes.

If liked, add nuts to butter, stirring for about 5 minutes before adding semolina.

halkoum

Turkish delight

MAKES 20 – 24

1.25 kg (2¾ lb) sugar
225 g (8 oz) glucose
1 litre (1¾ pints) water
175 g (6 oz) cornflour
juice of ½ lemon

30 ml (2 tbsp) rose water
2.5 ml (½ tsp) mastic
cochineal (optional)
60 g (2½ oz) chopped pistachios (or almonds)
icing sugar for dusting

Dissolve sugar and glucose in 250 ml (8 fl oz) of the water and bring to the boil, stirring every now and then. In another pot, put the cornflour and 700 ml (1¼ pints) water and stir well until smooth. Slowly bring to boiling point, stirring all the time, until the mixture is a smooth paste. The next step requires some care. Slowly add the cornflour paste to the glucose sugar water. Beating vigorously will cause it to become lumpy.

Bring to the boil again and leave uncovered over a very low heat for 3 hours. Stir occasionally with a wooden spoon. Make sure your mixture does not boil too fast, otherwise it will caramelize. This boiling process is very important for the recipe to be a success as the mixture must be the right consistency. It is ready when a little of the mixture, allowed to cool slightly then squeezed between two fingers, clings like toffee. Add the lemon juice and rose water, as well as the mastic, pounded with a little sugar. If you want colour, add a few drops of cochineal or other colouring. Stir vigorously and cook for 1 – 2 minutes longer.

Remove from the heat, add chopped nuts and mix well. Dust a baking tray with cornflour and pour in the mixture, smooth it with a spatula and leave to set for at least 24 hours. Cut into squares and dust with icing sugar. Turkish delight keeps well if stored in tins.

VARIATIONS

■ Here is a simpler, though not authentic, method.

MAKES 24

450 g (1 lb) gelatine
500 ml (17 fl oz) warm water
45 ml (3 tbsp) rose or orange blossom water

vanilla essence
100 g (4 oz) sugar
cornflour for dusting
icing sugar for dusting

Melt the gelatine in the warm water and simmer over a low heat for about 10 minutes, stirring all the time, until mixture thickens. Add rose or orange blossom water, vanilla essence and sugar, and cook for 1 minute. Dust a tray with cornflour and spread the mixture in it. Leave to cool. Cut into squares and roll in icing sugar. This mixture also keeps well.

■ If you want a nuttier version, after you have added the rose water, vanilla essence and sugar, hold a walnut or pecan half or whole blanched almond with a pair of cleaned tweezers or small kitchen tongs and dip into the Turkish delight mixture. Allow to set and dip again, repeating once more. After allowing to set, roll in icing sugar. This is well worth the trouble for a special occasion.

mirabba teen bi atr

green figs preserved in syrup

The figs must not be too ripe and must be unblemished. This preserve is delicious with toast and cream.

MAKES 1 X 400 ML (¾ PINT) JAR

1 kg (2¼ lb) figs
600 g (1¼ lb) sugar

500 ml (17 fl oz) water
15 – 30 ml (1 – 2 tbsp) lemon juice
15 ml (1 tbsp) orange blossom or rose water (optional)

Wash and trim stems of figs. Heat the sugar and water for about 5 minutes until dissolved. Add figs and bring syrup to the boil. Reduce heat and simmer gently until figs are fairly soft. Remove figs with slotted spoon and transfer to a warm, sterilized glass jar.

Check syrup and, if it is too thin, boil rapidly for a few minutes until thick enough to coat the back of a spoon. Flavour with lemon juice and orange blossom or rose water if using. Pour over figs and seal.

kerayz bi atr

cherry preserve

MAKES 1 X 400 ML (¾ PINT) JAR

1 kg (2¼ lb) cherries

1 kg (2¼ lb) sugar
15 ml (1 tbsp) lemon juice

Stone cherries and layer with sugar in a glass bowl. Leave overnight. Slowly bring to the boil in their own liquid. Simmer very gently until soft (about 20 minutes), stirring often. Add the lemon juice. If you think that the syrup is too thin, remove the cherries and boil the liquid until it thickens. Once the syrup is of the right consistency pour the preserve into a warm, sterilized glass jar and seal.

halawet semsem

sesame snaps

MAKES 18

450 g (1 lb) sugar

450 g (1 lb) sesame seeds

Combine sesame seeds and sugar in a saucepan and stir continuously at a very low temperature until the sugar has dissolved and the mixture turns slightly brown. Pour mixture into a greased tray. Spread to 5 mm (¼ in) thickness and slice with a sharp knife while still warm. When the mixture cools, it becomes brittle. Wrap in greaseproof paper.

loz

almond drops

MAKES 18

125 g (4½ oz) icing sugar, sifted
75 ml (3 fl oz) orange blossom water

125 g (4½ oz) ground almonds

Combine the ground almonds with the icing sugar and orange blossom water. It should form a stiff paste – add an additional tablespoon of orange blossom water, if necessary. Shape into small balls and roll in icing sugar. You can press a pistachio nut or a piece of almond into the balls, if you like.

mishmish

apricot delights

SERVES 25 – 30

about 15 g (½ oz) icing sugar to taste
nuts, finely chopped (optional)

225 g (8 oz) dried apricots

sugar (optional)

Chop apricots finely. Add enough icing sugar to suit your taste. Have a basin of water handy. Knead apricots, wetting hands occasionally, until you have a smooth, moist paste. Shape into small balls. You can leave them like this or you can make a little hollow and fill it with finely chopped nuts, mixed with a little sugar (pistachios are good). Close the opening and roll in icing sugar. For pretty presentation, serve in little paper cups.

makroun bi loz

macaroons with nuts

MAKES 45 – 50

450 g (1 lb) plain flour
5 ml (1 tsp) salt
10 ml (2 tsp) baking powder
100 g (4 oz) softened butter (clarified
   if possible)

250 ml (8 fl oz) water
200 g (7 oz) walnuts, minced
vegetable oil for deep-frying
chilled syrup (see p. 128)

Sift flour, salt and baking powder together. With your fingers, rub the butter into the dry ingredients until the mixture is crumbly. Add water and mix with a knife to a firm dough.

Take one small piece at a time and roll into a long rope about the thickness of your finger (not too fat, not too thin). Cut into 5-cm (2-in) pieces. Take each piece and press firmly downwards with the back of a knife to form a boat shape. Fill the boat with minced walnuts and pinch closed.

Fry in hot oil until golden and immediately drop into cold syrup to absorb the sweetness.

safarjal

quince titbits

MAKES 30

1 kg (2¼ lb) quinces
450 g (1 lb) sugar

125 ml (4 fl oz) water
30 ml (2 tbsp) lemon juice
pistachios or walnuts for decoration

Wash and quarter quinces, leaving pith, pips and skin. Put in a saucepan and simmer slowly in their own juices for about 30 minutes. If they are dry, add a little warm water until they soften. Liquidize or force through a strainer and reserve.

Dissolve the sugar in the water and cook for about 5 minutes, until the syrup has thickened. Add the lemon juice and quince mixture. Simmer over a very low heat, stirring all the time, until the mixture thickens and comes away from the bottom of the pan. Spread out on a tray and leave to dry for a few days.

Cut into traditional diamond shapes or squares, decorate with a nut on each square and serve with coffee. You can also put half the mixture into the tray, spread over a layer of nuts, add the balance of the paste and leave to set.

refreshing drinks

STREET VENDORS ARE a common sight in Lebanon, selling all kinds of delicious things to eat and drink. The lemonade vendors serve your drink in a glass which is then rinsed and used to serve the next person.

Lovely drinks can be had at any time, very different from the soft drinks one gets elsewhere. The custom of soft drinks being served at all times of the day is still traditional amongst Lebanese communities, so do not be surprised if you visit and, before you are served tea or coffee, a tray of different soft drinks is passed around. One of the nicest drinks is watered-down yoghurt, to which dried mint is added.

sharab bizr shumman

melon seed mead

MAKES 500 ML (17 FL OZ)

seeds of 1 melon

500 ml (17 fl oz) water
sugar, to taste
2.5 ml (½ tsp) easy-blend dried yeast

Pound melon seeds to a pulp. Dissolve in water in a muslin bag, until water looks milky. Add sugar to taste. Add powdered yeast and stir well until dissolved. Stand for a few hours before serving.

ayran laban

mint yoghurt

The usual mixture is equal quantities of yoghurt and water. If you only want to make one drink, only half a cup of water to half a cup of yoghurt is required. It is deliciously refreshing.

MAKES 600 ML (1 PINT)

300 ml (½ pint) plain yoghurt

300 ml (½ pint) water
salt to taste
15 – 30 ml (1 – 2 tbsp) dried mint

Beat yoghurt with a rotary beater or vigorously with a wooden spoon, add water and beat further. You can also use a liquidizer or blender. Add a little salt to taste. Crush the mint between the palms of your hands and add to mixture. Refrigerate or add ice and serve immediately.

haleeb el loz

almond drink

MAKES 550 ML (17 ½ FL OZ)

225 g (8 oz) almonds

500 ml (17 fl oz) water

30 ml (2 tbsp) orange blossom water (optional)

450 g (1 lb) sugar, or to taste

Put almonds, water and orange blossom water, if using, in a pan and simmer for about 10 minutes. Drain, reserving liquid. Skin the almonds by pressing between finger and thumb – they will pop out of their skins easily. Pound the nuts or liquidize to a fine pulp. Add the sugar to the reserved water and bring to the boil, adding more sugar or water as necessary.

Tie the almonds in a muslin bag. Remove water from heat. Place the bag in the water and leave to soak, squeezing the bag occasionally until most of the contents are dissolved. Refrigerate before serving or serve with ice.

sharbat safarjal

quince syrup

**MAKES 600 – 750 ML (18 FL OZ –
1¼ PINTS)**

2 fresh quinces

600 – 750 ml (18 fl oz – 1¼ pints) water

125 ml (4 fl oz) fresh lemon juice

450 g (1 lb) sugar

Slice quinces very thinly or grate, first removing the pips and the pith. As you cut them, put the quinces in a bowl with half the water, add 30 ml (2 tbsp) of the lemon juice. This will prevent the fruit from discolouring. Drain quinces and wrap in a double thickness of muslin. Squeeze over a bowl to extract as much juice as possible. Discard remaining pulp.

Slowly bring the rest of the water and sugar to the boil, stirring constantly until the sugar has dissolved. Increase the heat and boil rapidly for 5 minutes. Add quince juice and the remaining lemon juice. Simmer for a further 5 minutes, stirring all the time. Cool. To serve, add about 90 ml (3½ fl oz) water to 90 ml (3½ fl oz) syrup and fill glass with crushed ice.

sharbat rivas

rhubarb sherbet

MAKES 600 – 750 ML (18 FL OZ – 1¼ PINTS)

250 ml (8 fl oz) water
450 g (1 lb) sugar

1 rhubarb stalk

Wash rhubarb well, trim and cut into pieces. Bring water and rhubarb to the boil in an enamel or stainless-steel saucepan. Turn heat to low and simmer about 20 minutes. Sieve the pulp and water into a bowl, forcing as much pulp through as possible. Discard what is left. Alternatively, liquidize. Measure juice and return to saucepan, making up to 300 ml (½ pint) with water. Add sugar and slowly bring to the boil, stirring rapidly until sugar has dissolved. Increase heat and boil rapidly, undisturbed, for 5 minutes. Cool. To serve, add 90 ml (3½ fl oz) syrup to 90 ml (3½ fl oz) water, stir and fill glass with crushed ice.

sharbat ettute

mulberry syrup

very ripe mulberries
sugar

lemon juice
water

Liquidize mulberries then strain, or force through a fine strainer with a wooden spoon. Measure liquid and put into an enamel or stainless-steel saucepan. Add double the amount of sugar and some lemon juice. Slowly bring to the boil, stirring until sugar dissolves. Increase heat and boil rapidly for 5 minutes. Cool. Store in sterilized bottles. To serve add 15 ml (1 tbsp) mulberry juice to one glass of iced water.

sharbat maward

rose water syrup

MAKES 300 ML (10 FL OZ)

400 g (14 oz) sugar
250 ml (8 fl oz) water

15 ml (1 tbsp) lemon juice
30 ml (2 tbsp) rose water
cochineal

Put sugar, water and lemon juice in a pan and slowly bring to the boil, stirring until the sugar dissolves. Increase heat and boil rapidly for 5 minutes. Add rose water and enough cochineal to turn syrup pink. Cool and preserve in sterilized bottles. Add to iced water to serve.

sharbat mazaher

orange blossom water syrup

MAKES 300 ML (10 FL OZ)

400 g (14 oz) sugar
250 ml (8 fl oz) water

15 ml (1 tbsp) lemon juice
45 ml (3 tbsp) orange blossom water
2 – 3 cloves

Put sugar, water and lemon juice in a pan and slowly bring to the boil, stirring until the sugar dissolves. Increase heat and boil rapidly for 5 minutes until thick. Add orange blossom water. Bring to the boil once more. Turn heat down to low and simmer for 30 minutes. Remove pan from heat and leave overnight. Bring to the boil once again and simmer for 30 minutes. Stir in the cloves. Pour into warm, sterilized containers. Cool and seal.

hot drinks

ALL THE FOLLOWING can be added to ordinary tea, or just pour boiling water on the leaves or dried herbs, adding sugar to taste. Serve very hot.

sha ib itr
rose geranium tea

For each cup, add tea or boiling water to a handful of fresh, washed geranium leaves or about 5 ml (1 tsp) dried, crushed leaves.

shay ib na 'na
mint tea

For each cup of tea, use 5 ml (1 tsp) dried mint or a few fresh leaves.

shay ou irfeh
cinnamon tea

Add a little cinnamon powder to a cup of hot black tea and add sugar to taste.

shay ib yansoun
aniseed tea

Add 2.5 ml (½ tsp) of ground aniseed to a cup of hot black tea and sugar to taste.

VARIATION
■ You can also use sage, basil, jasmine, marjoram or rose petals to make tea.

sahlab soukhon

hot cornflour drink

Boil enough milk to fill 1 large mug, with sugar to taste. Add 5 ml (1 tsp) cornflour mixed with a little cold milk and made into a smooth paste. Simmer for a while, stirring all the time. Serve hot, sprinkled with a little cinnamon, if desired.

Lebanese coffee

A Turkish proverb:
Coffee should be: *Black as Hell, Strong as Death, and Sweet as Love.*

Now for the supreme drink, served at any time under so many different names – Turkish coffee, Arabic coffee, Greek coffee and Lebanese coffee. It has been drunk since the fifteenth century. Legend has it that coffee was discovered by a goat-herdsman who noticed that his goats didn't sleep after eating the red berries of the coffee bush. It is said that this drink aids digestion and lends a pleasant atmosphere, especially after a meal.

Coffee is also served to welcome visitors on their arrival. Yet another occasion is after a funeral, when friends and relatives are immediately served with coffee on returning to the house, usually prepared by someone left behind to ensure that everything goes smoothly and efficiently. This is followed by pies and other savoury offerings. Of course, when making such a large amount of coffee, a large saucepan must be used. To work out quantities a good rule of thumb to follow is 1 heaped teaspoon of coffee to 1 small coffee cup of water and 1 teaspoon of sugar for each cup. The coffee is normally made in a *racwhih*, a copper container with a long handle.

MAKES 1 CUP

6 ml (1 tsp) ground coffee, heaped

1 small coffee cup water
5 ml (1 tsp) sugar

For each person, measure the quantities above into the copper container or a saucepan and heat gently. Once on the stove, do not leave unattended as it easily rises to the top and overflows, resulting in quite a mess. The coffee must not bubble, so as soon as it starts to rise, remove from the heat and, when it settles, put it back on the stove, repeating this procedure three times.

Into each cup add a little of the foam and slowly pour the coffee so as not to disturb the foam. It is considred impolite to serve the coffee to the guests without the foam. Do not stir the coffee as you will disturb the grains that have settled on the bottom and, of course, the foam. Serve on a tray with a few glasses of cold water. If you have only a few guests, you may ask them if they desire sweet, medium or unsweetened coffee and make them individually.

To end an evening of Lebanese entertainment the marghile (pipe) is passed around. The marghile cools the smoke by passing it through water in a flexible pipe.

Lebanese coffee (above) served with Turkish delight (p. 148).

measurements

approximate cup and spoon measures

250 ml	1 cup
190 ml	¾ cup
125 ml	½ cup
80 ml	⅓ cup
60 ml	¼ cup
15 ml	1 tablespoon
5 ml	1 teaspoon
3 ml	¾ teaspoon
2 ml	½ teaspoon
1 ml	¼ teaspoon

approximate weight measures

30 g	1 oz
60 g	2 oz
85 g	3 oz
115 g	4 oz
140 g	5 oz
170 g	6 oz
200 g	7 oz
230 g	8 oz
450 g	1 lb
900 g	2 lb

glossary

adas lentil
aegga omelette
ahwah coffee
al-moukabbalat hors d'œuvres
arnabeet cauliflower
a-tayif, a'ta-ef pancakes
atr syrup
avokaeta avocado pear
aweimat fritters
ayran mint
aysh shami Lebanese bread
bahlearwah filo pastry
balah date
balouza cornflour
bamiey, bamja okra
banadoura, banadura tomato
basal, basali onions
baskaweet biscuits
bata duck
batatas, batatah, batatis, ba'ta'tis potatoes
batenghen aubergine
bayd egg
bisella pea
burghal wheat
dajah chicken
djegh poultry, chicken
d'megh brains
eishta thick cream
fasoulya beans
fa'tay'yeh pies
fawikih fruit
filfil helw sweet peppers
fil-forn baked or roasted
ful bean
gambari prawns
gebna cheese
gham'mee tripe
gh'dra vegetables
habash turkey
halawaiyaet sweetmeats
haleeb milk
haûh prunes
hindbeh endive/chicory/frisée-lettuce
hoummus chickpeas
'inaeb grapes
kabees pickles
kafta, kafte rissoles or meatballs
karrat, koraat leek
kashi, kashih, kibda liver
kelwaewi kidney
kerayz cherry
khal vinegar
khijaar, kh'yaar, kj'yaar cucumber
kh'odar, khodar vegetables
khoubz bread
knafie cookies

koronb cabbage
kousa courgettes
kreem cream
kroueen trotters
krush tripe
laban yoghurt
labneh cheese
lagham meat
laghma lamb
lamoun lemon or orange
l'ft turnips
loobyea kho'dar green beans
l'orse potato
loubien butter bean
loz nuts, almonds
mahshi stuffed
mai-mal-ha brine
malfouf cabbage
maqli fried
mashwi, mishwi grilled
maward rose water
mazaher orange blossom water
mezze hors d'oeuvres
mirabba teen green figs
mishmish apricots
mowz banana
riz rice
safarjal quince
salatah salads
samak fish
shaanegh, spenegh spinach
semsem sesame
sharbat refreshing drinks
shirreeyeh vermicelli
shorbah soup
sukker sugar
tahini sesame sauce
teen figs
warah einab vine leaves
yaghni stews
yansoun aniseed
zatoon olives
zhouret hot drinks

index